History of the
SOVIET UNION

DANTES/DSST* Test Study Guide

All rights reserved. This Study Guide, Book and Flashcards are protected under the US Copyright Law. No part of this book or study guide or flashcards may be reproduced, distributed or stored in a retrieval system, or transmitted in any form or by any means, electronic, mechanical, photocopying, recording, or otherwise, without the prior written permission of the publisher Breely Crush Publishing, LLC.

© 2026 Breely Crush Publishing, LLC

DSST is a registered trademark of The Thomson Corporation and its affiliated companies, and does not endorse this book.

971010620143

Copyright ©2003 - 2026, Breely Crush Publishing, LLC.

All rights reserved.

This Study Guide, Book and Flashcards are protected under the US Copyright Law. No part of this publication may be reproduced, distributed or stored in a retrieval system, or transmitted in any form or by any means, electronic, mechanical, photocopying, recording, or otherwise, without the prior written permission of the publisher Breely Crush Publishing, LLC.

Published by Breely Crush Publishing, LLC
10808 River Front Parkway
South Jordan, UT 84095
www.breelycrushpublishing.com

ISBN-10: 1-61433-669-5
ISBN-13: 978-1-61433-669-3

Printed and bound in the United States of America.

*DSST is a registered trademark of The Thomson Corporation and its affiliated companies, and does not endorse this book.

 Table of Contents

Section 1: Russia Under the Old Regime 1
    Section 1.1: Governing Institutions 1
    Section 1.2: Economics 3
    Section 1.3: Culture and Society 4
    Section 1.4: Foreign Affairs 4
    Section 1.5: Revolutionary Movement 6

Section 2: The Revolutionary Period 1914-1921 9
    Section 2.1: The First World War 9
    Section 2.2: February/March Revolution 11
    Section 2.3: Interim 12
    Section 2.4: Bolshevik Revolution 12
    Section 2.5: Civil War 15
    Section 2.6: New Economic Policy (NEP) 16

Section 3: Pre-War Stalinism 17
    Section 3.1: Lenin's Successor 17
    Section 3.2: Collectivization 18
    Section 3.3: Industrialization 20
    Section 3.4: Reign of Terror 21
    Section 3.5: Culture 24
    Section 3.6: Nationalities 26

Section 4: The Second World War 26
    Section 4.1: Pre-war Foreign Relations 26
    Section 4.2: The Course of the War 29
    Section 4.3: The Impact of the War 34
    Section 4.4: Settlements of WWII and the Origins of the Cold War 34

Section 5: Post-war Stalinism 36
    Section 5.1: Reconstruction 36
    Section 5.2: Nationalism 38
    Section 5.3: Arms Race 39
    Section 5.4: Cold War in Europe 39
    Section 5.5: Cold War in Asia 43

Section 6: The Khrushchev Years 44
    Section 6.1: Succession Struggle 44
    Section 6.2: De-Stalinization 45
    Section 6.3: Soviet Relations with the U.S. Under Khrushchev 46
    Section 6.4: Rift with China 49
    Section 6.5: Change of Power 50
    Section 6.6: Proxy Wars 52
    Section 6.7: War in Afghanistan 52

Section 7: Reform and Collapse 54
    Section 7.1: Global Challengers 54
    Section 7.2: External Factors (Afghanistan, Islam) 57
    Section 7.3: Perestroika and Glasnost 57
    Section 7.4: Reemergence of the Nationalities Issue 65
    Section 7.5: Revolutions in Eastern Europe 67
    Section 7.6: End of the Union of Soviet Socialist Republics 70
    Section 7.7: Gorbachev's Legacy 71
Sample Test Questions 72
Test-Taking Strategies 102
Test Preparation 102
Legal Note 103

 Section 1: Russia Under the Old Regime

For much of its history, Russia both identified with, and stood apart from, European nations. While admiring European culture from afar, the country struggled with its poor masses and large geographical spaces. The country took various approaches to dealing with its troubles. Leaders oscillated between enacting reforms and continuing oppression. While serfdom was abolished in 1861, the majority of Russians did not see any concrete benefit from this act.

As Russia entered the twentieth century, it could no longer hide from the social changes that had swept through other regions of the world. Unlike other nations that were able to provide upward mobility and middle class standing to broader swathes of the population, Russia's masses faced very few opportunities. These circumstances left the country ripe for change.

SECTION 1.1: GOVERNING INSTITUTIONS

The government that would eventually meet its demise in the 1917 February Revolution began in 1721. The Russian Empire existed for almost two hundred years and had stood as one of the largest empires the world had ever seen. For nearly the entire existence of the Russian Empire, the country was an absolute monarchy. This meant a monarch exercised complete control over the nation. In the case of the Russian Empire, this absolute monarch was called the tsar (pronounced zar). The word *tsar* had its root in the Latin word "Caesar."

Tsar Alexander II, who ruled Russia for nearly thirty years, embarked on significant reforms for the Russian nation. For much of his reign, the ruler sought peace for his nation. He was also a relatively liberal leader, concerned about enacting reforms that would benefit the average Russian. This tsar wanted to spur economic growth, and passed reforms that would allow more freedom for industry and commerce. Importantly, Alexander II liberated the serfs in 1861. Despite his openness to change, an assassin supporting a socialist organization killed Tsar Alexander in 1881.

The assassination of Tsar Alexander II deeply influenced his son who became Tsar Alexander III. For the remainder of the Romanov dynasty, the monarchs would fear assassination. Tsar Alexander III was not as liberal as his father had been, and lived by the maxim "Orthodoxy, Autocracy, and Nationality." Instead of continuing his father's liberal policies, the new tsar tried to overturn some of them. He weakened local institutions, mandated Russian language instruction, and surrounded himself with very conservative advisors.

At the turn of the twentieth century, the absolute monarchy was resting on the weak shoulders of Tsar Nicholas II who had ascended to the throne after Tsar Alexander III's death in 1894. Tsar Nicholas faced complex problems that would have taxed the skills of any leader, but he was ill-equipped to handle the challenges. The nation faced a variety of problems. Russia was still adjusting to the liberation of the serfs. Institutions and customs failed to help these individuals succeed in their newfound freedom. At the same time, non-Russian populations were losing patience with the oppressive Russification that had begun under Tsar Alexander III. Those Russians who had migrated to urban areas and were becoming the basis of Russian industrial growth felt ignored by the government while being exploited by businesses. Additionally, new ideas were sifting into the national mind as new policies allowed for the spread of liberal ideas through the institutions of higher education.

While the social and economic forces worked against the weak tsar's authority, revolutionary groups began to organize themselves. In 1898, proponents of new ideas started the Social Democratic Party in Minsk. Eduard Bernstein, a confirmed follower of Marxism, played a large role in the party's founding. This party would eventually give birth to the Soviet Union's communist party. The Social Democratic Party espoused the belief that the urban workers, or proletariat, would be crucial to effecting the transition to socialism in Russia.

As the party organized itself, leaders began publishing influential pamphlets. Foreshadowing his future role, Vladimir Ilyich Ulyanov, better known as Vladimir Lenin, wrote a highly influential article in 1902 titled *What Is to Be Done?* The pamphlet gave practical direction to the efforts of the revolutionaries. The name of the pamphlet came from a novel with the same name. The novel told the story of a woman gaining her economic independence, and the story was meant as an allegory to show how Russian society could solve its problems through the implementation of socialist ideals. It comes as no surprise that the author, Nikolai Chernyshevsky, who espoused such radical ideas, wrote the novel from prison, and would languish for years in Siberia. The novel would become more notorious for the revolutionary writing it would inspire.

Lenin's article pushed for the organization of the party to focus and direct the actions of the proletariat. Concerned that workers would become apathetic when left to their own devices and that they might embrace smaller reforms like the formation of trade unions, Lenin pushed for the organization of a party that would foment true socialism. Lenin was preoccupied with the idea that the workers would not have the intellectual capacity to bring socialism in its purist form to the country.

Lenin's aggressive stance in the article influenced and promoted a split in the growing movement. The Russian Social Democratic Labor Party (RSDLP) became divided between the Bolsheviks and the Mensheviks in 1903. On one side, with Lenin as the leader, were the Bolsheviks. With a name taken from the Russian word for "majority,"

Lenin's Bolsheviks advocated aggressive and even violent measures to promote change in the Russian Empire. The other faction splitting from the RSDLP was the Mensheviks. The name of this faction came from the Russian word for "minority." The Mensheviks, headed by Julius Martov, espoused a different path toward socialism. Ironically, at the time of the split, the Bolsheviks may well have been in the minority. The Mensheviks did not advocate for a direct jump to pure socialism. Instead, they argued that the Russian proletariat would need a time of transition from its current state through democratic rule to socialism. The Bolsheviks had no patience for this view.

SECTION 1.2: ECONOMICS

The economic situation of the average Russian at the turn of the century was dire. Although the government had hoped to benefit from serfs who became landholders and vested in the society, serfs generally did not receive enough land to provide for themselves. Also, the way in which the land had been given to the former serfs prevented them from selling or mortgaging the land. These practices severely inhibited the average person from improving their economic position. It was not uncommon to have masses of the poor riot just because they were looking for enough food to subsist. While the government initiated studies to find out why there were such severe food shortages, no solutions could be agreed upon. The nation was simply not producing enough food to feed its growing population and the lack of sufficient food production led to the importation of goods. Tax revenues went down as people faced economic hardship, but the national debt grew as the empire strained to import the products that it needed for its bellies and its military.

The individual Russian faced great personal hardship, and a severe famine ravaged the land from 1891 until 1892. Among other forces, this famine illustrated the need for economic change that socialism would promise to bring. In 1891, atypical weather patterns at the start of the growing season, followed by a dry summer, devastated the crops. Lack of rain triggered the death of livestock and plants. Exacerbated by the famine, cholera spread. The cost in lives stood at nearly a half million people.

The government made a bad situation worse by suppressing media coverage of the disaster and by not improving infrastructure that could have been used to channel resources from other parts of the country to the affected areas. The famous author, Leo Tolstoy, directly blamed the government and the Russian Orthodox Church.

The industrial situation was also abysmal, although Finance Minister Sergei Witte had attempted to spur industrial growth. Witte had tried to improve the economic situation through policies meant to attract foreign investors who would then pour capital into the nation that needed to industrialize. Witte focused on improving communications and railways. He even tried to introduce a meritocracy when most government posts had been filled through personal connections.

Facing many of the problems that other countries had experienced in their industrial revolutions, the Russian worker dealt with long hours, unsafe conditions, and unfair labor practices. Where many workers had hoped that their move to urban areas would improve their lives, they were disappointed, leaving them ripe for receiving the socialist message. As discontented workers turned to political action, the government responded by cracking down.

SECTION 1.3: CULTURE AND SOCIETY

Adding to the issues faced by the weak tsar, the bulk of Russian society at the turn of the century was in the peasant class. Between 80% and 82% of the population fell into this class. The upper class was in the lower double digits—between 12% and 13%. A paltry 5% or so of society could call itself middle class. While the aristocracy patronized artists such as Tchaikovsky and Fabergé, the rest of the people in the country were on the verge of starving. Literacy before the 1917 revolution was well under 20%, with women being far less literate than their male counterparts.

Despite the illiteracy of the majority of the Russian people, Russian literature entered a Golden Age during the middle of the 1800s. Notable authors appeared in all the genres. Alexander Pushkin's art signaled the beginning of the golden age of Russian poetry. Pushkin's works ranged from shorter poems to novels composed of verses. His favored themes included revenge, honor, and mortality as seen in Russian society of his time. Leo Tolstoy and Fyodor Dostoyevsky treated the genre of prose, and Anton Chekhov mastered the short story and drama genres.

SECTION 1.4: FOREIGN AFFAIRS

Russian foreign affairs also suffered during the turn of the century. The Russo-Japanese War would tax Russian resources and lead to an embarrassing outcome. Stemming from the rivalry between the Russian Empire and the Japanese Empire (an empire very much on an ascending arc), the two countries would dispute ownership of Manchuria and Korea. With the majority of the conflict taking place in Southern Manchuria, operations took place on the Liaodong Peninsula and Mukden, and the seas around Korea, Japan, and the Yellow Sea. Russia's chronic underestimation of the Japanese would lead to their defeat.

Handicapped by its northern location, the Russian port of Vladivostok was trapped by ice during much of the year. Russian merchant and navy ships could only access the port during the summer months. Both civilian and military operations faced challenges due to the geography of Vladivostok. Strategically, Russia needed a Pacific Ocean warm water port. The Russians wanted to improve their lot by acquiring Port Arthur, a Chinese port, to the south. The power that could control Port Arthur would possess an asset in that the port could be used all year long.

After Japan prevailed over China in the First Sino-Japanese War, Japan did not feel any need to negotiate with the Russians through 1903. Japan understood the strategic importance of dominating the Korean peninsula. Japan's position was to allow Russia to control Manchuria, while Japan would continue dominating the Korean peninsula.

In 1904, the countries ended negotiations. Foreshadowing future acts, the Japanese launched a surprise attack on the Russian fleet that was floating in Port Arthur. The Russian fleet never recovered momentum, and Tsar Nicholas II acted under the illusion that the Russian fleet was superior to the Japanese. Instead of ending the war before losses mounted, the tsar insisted on continuing the conflict, incurring huge losses of both personnel and materiel. The global community was aghast as Japan absolutely dominated the Russian forces. The momentum gained by the Japanese Empire would shift the balance of power in the region and have long-lasting consequences, not only in the region but across the world in the decades to come.

The tsar refused to accept the reality that his forces were being routed at every turn. He refused opportunity after opportunity to withdraw his forces from the conflict. Although the Japanese struggled to maintain their own military because of their chronic lack of resources, a problem that would rear its head later in World War II, they were thrilled to be winning every engagement.

From February 20, 1905 to March 10, 1905, the two sides engaged in the Battle of Mukden. This would be the turning point of the war that would lead the Japanese to conclude that the conflict should end sooner rather than later. Fought on land, the battle would be one of the largest battles fought prior to World War I. The Japanese forces were outnumbered. Imperial Japanese forces fielded about 270,000 soldiers, while the Russians numbered about 340,000. In total, about 610,000 combatants fought, and the sides together incurred around 164,000 casualties. The Japanese gained an advantage when the Russians failed to move their forces in an orderly fashion. Eventually, they were able to encircle a large swathe of the Russian forces, motivating the Russians to retreat. Although the battle ended with the Japanese having driven the Russians from the city of Mukden, both armies had paid dearly.

The Japanese determined that protracted conflict was not in their interest, and looked to end the conflict. Theodore Roosevelt negotiated a peace agreement between the two sides which was known as the Treaty of Portsmouth. On September 5, 1905, Russia and Japan signed the agreement. The humiliating defeat at the hands of the Japanese irreparably damaged the tsar's and the government's credibility. The people were losing patience with their ineffective government that was mired in corruption. The war added one more straw to the back of a camel that would soon collapse.

SECTION 1.5: REVOLUTIONARY MOVEMENT

Leading up to 1905, the people were pushing for more freedom as they lost faith in their government. They had suffered famine, oppression, and now international embarrassment at the hands of the Japanese. Workers were striking, demanding better treatment. Several different political groups were entering the national consciousness. Some groups were calling for a constitutional monarchy. The Union of Zemstvo Constitutionalists and the Union of Liberation were among these. The socialists fell into two main camps, the Socialist Revolutionary Party and the Russian Social Democratic Labor Party.

The political unrest that resulted in the 1905 Russian Revolution appeared in a variety of ways and affected large segments of the empire. Sometimes, the people's frustration directly targeted the government, while at other times it had no direction. This unrest was manifested as terrorism, strikes among the urban workers, unrest among the peasants, and mutinies in the military. As demands for change increased, including demands for a legislature, the tsar tried to implement some changes but nothing as sweeping as establishing a national legislature.

The event that would become known as Bloody Sunday would accelerate the coming revolution. St. Petersburg experienced growing strikes in December of 1904. As the numbers of strikers grew, the city faced the loss of electricity, media services, and use of public areas. On Sunday, January 22, 1905, when workers organized a march on the tsar's Winter Palace in an effort to bring their grievances directly to their "Little Father," soldiers guarding the palace opened fire. Anywhere from two hundred to a thousand people died in this tragic event.

Bloody Sunday inspired strikes throughout every industrialized part of the Russian Empire. Along with the strikes came other massacres. The government was so alarmed that it closed educational institutions in March of 1905, hoping to put a stop to the simmering rebellion. The strikes reached massive proportions toward the end of the year. Over two million workers were on strike by October 26, 1905. Additionally, the nation's railways had ground to a halt.

While the nation's industries were not functioning, the military also faced challenges. As noted before, the war against Japan ended with the signing of the Treaty of Portsmouth late in 1905. The Russian navy had faced a bloody and embarrassing war. As the war came to a close, sailors mutinied in multiple locations: Sevastopol, Vladivostok, and Kronstadt. Famously, the crew of the Potemkin, a battleship in the Black Sea, mutinied and took control of the ship.

Desperate to end the chaos, Tsar Nicholas II issued the October Manifesto in October 1905. This document was dramatic as it showed that Nicholas was so impressed by events that he was considering giving up the absolute monarchy in favor of a constitutional monarchy that many other nations had already adopted.

The October Manifesto attempted to stem the tide of the revolution by promising more rights and a national legislative body called the Duma. The Duma was to have the approval authority for all laws to be enacted in the empire. Unfortunately, the Duma could still be trumped by the tsar. The tsar had the veto power over the Duma. Although the revolution would provide limited relief, it led to the establishment of the limited constitutional monarchy, the State Duma of the Russian Empire, the multi-party system, and the Russian Constitution of 1906.

The Duma did not accomplish anything of lasting effect. In part, it accomplished little because it did not meet for very long. The Duma was also struggling because many of the agitators for change, like the socialists, refused to participate. The socialists did not view the Duma's creation as radical enough and did not submit any candidates for election. Also, the Russian establishment had reason to oppose the Duma, as the elected body wanted to strip away power from the establishment in favor of land reform that would give more freedom to the peasants.

The Manifesto did help to end the strikes and economic turmoil temporarily, but soon repression began. Only a few months after the Manifesto was issued, the government began executing opponents, and military law was put in place over large parts of the empire in the years to follow.

From 1906 until 1911, Russia felt the influence of Peter Stolypin, who would have a large influence over agricultural policies in the empire. Stolypin was Nicholas II's Chairman of the Council of Ministers—the Prime Minister of Russia—from 1906 to 1911. Stolypin inherited a nearly untenable position. While trying to deal with the radicals, he also had to face the economic problems of the empire. He was the rare leader of the empire during the period leading up to World War I who had both a systematic agenda and the energy to try to make lasting and effective reforms. Much of Stolypin's work focused on reforms that would grow the non-existent middle class in Russia. He hoped to achieve this through giving peasants a private property interest. As mentioned before, the system under which the Russian peasant existed did not favor the regular person being able to sell or mortgage their own property. Thus, upward mobility was nearly impossible. Stolypin and his cohorts saw that change could be effected by merging the scattered plots of land. He also proposed practices that would provide banking institutions to peasants or allow them to move to less populated lands. His encouragement of capitalist practices inflamed both the socialists and the traditional monarchists who opposed changes to the old system. Stolypin also dabbled in granting religious freedom to marginalized groups, such as the Jews, and in providing social welfare programs to workers.

However, there was also a darker side to Stolypin. Stolypin was notorious for his handling of the rebellious situation he had inherited after the Revolution of 1905. As detailed above, the nation was more or less in anarchy. Massive swathes of the infrastructure were affected by strikes, and assassinations and violence toward government officials was commonplace. In fact, Stolypin himself, as well as his family, were injured in various assassination attempts. Stolypin's response to these threats was to enact harsh martial law. His new reforms on the legal front allowed for efficient and swift consequences to those viewed as threats to the establishment. What few protections had been available before Stolypin were dispensed with. Those opposing the monarchy could expect speedy arrest, trial, and summary execution. At least three thousand faced execution under Stolypin's tenure. His version of justice was so harsh that his name became associated with the noose and with the railroad cars that transported prisoners to Siberia.

The full potential or eventual outcome of Stolypin's career would never be known. On September 1, 1911, Stolypin was attending the theatre in Kiev, Ukraine. A socialist assassin named Dmitry Bogrov shot the controversial statesman just as the tsar was entering his own box in the theatre. Stolypin died three days later, and with the statesman died any organized vision for reforming the country. No other leader would commit to the changes that would threaten the absolute monarchy.

The Romanov Dynasty celebrated its Tercentenary—its three-hundred-year anniversary—in February 1913. Tsar Nicholas II and his family participated in an elaborate ceremony and lavish celebrations. The family traced the journey of the first Romanov after he had been elected king in 1613, journeying to towns that held significance to the Romanov family. The tsar imagined that such celebrations might stir the people to a fond remembrance of himas their "Little Father." Despite this fantastic propaganda opportunity, very few bought into this extravagant tribute to the past. The chaos in Russia was only growing, and no remembrance of the past glory could save the languishing dynasty now held loosely by Tsar Nicholas II.

By the dawning of World War I, Russia was still a country embroiled in poverty with little to no middle class. While the economy had seen some growth that approached double digits at the end of the 19th century, that growth slowed to about 5% after 1900. Every part of the economy felt the strain of political uncertainty as the monarchy refused to budge despite being faced with persistent resistance. As Russia faced the massive mobilization of her military that would take place in World War I, the weaknesses in the economy would soon be manifested.

 # Section 2: The Revolutionary Period 1914-1921

SECTION 2.1: THE FIRST WORLD WAR

Before entering into the circumstances that ended in Russia's involvement in the First World War, it would be important to view the cost that the war would impose on the Russian people. By the end of the war, over 3.3 million Russians would die, which included over 1.8 million military personnel and over 1.5 million civilians.

Although Tsar Nicholas II did not have a firm grip on internal matters, he still favored Russian expansion. Russia was facing off against Austria-Hungary in an ongoing dispute over the Balkans. Austria-Hungary was aligned with Germany as part of the German-formed alliance, termed the Triple Alliance. Along with Austria-Hungary and Italy, Germany pledged to support any one of the alliance that should be attacked by France or Russia. Russia, Britain, and France formed the opposition to the Triple Alliance. The tsar was determined to preserve or expand his own territory in the face of the threat.

Not all Russians welcomed a confrontation with the major European powers. Sergei Witte, an able organizer and the diplomat who had helped to negotiate the end to the Russo-Japanese War, saw the possibility of war as disastrous for the Russian Empire. Witte had urged the tsar to consider sweeping changes to the structure of the government and the economy even in 1905. Witte had also at other times warned the tsar that the nation was on the verge of collapse unless the tsar enacted the October Manifesto of 1905. Witte firmly opposed the war from the start, and many other important Russians agreed with him.

July 1914 would prove to be a trying time for practical men like Witte who realized that the Russian economy could not support the industrial military complex that would be levied against the Russian Empire by the Triple Alliance. On June 27, 1914, Archduke Franz Ferdinand and his wife were assassinated by a Serbian nationalist. The archduke had been the heir to the Austro-Hungarian throne and, as a consequence of the assassination, Austria-Hungary went to war against Serbia in July 28, 1914. This was the beginning of World War I. France sent a delegation to Russia even before Austria-Hungary did to secure Russia's support. Both countries hoped that perhaps Serbia would just accept Austria-Hungary's demands rather than go to war. In the end, neither Witte nor Rasputin could keep Russia out of the war.

At the start of the war, Russian boasted one of the largest armies that had ever been fielded; however, just as Witte and others had feared, the lack of Russian industry crippled the army from the start. While the army might have had around five million soldiers, it was equipped with fewer than 4.6 million rifles. Additionally, Russia's underdeveloped infrastructure would not allow the army to mobilize rapidly. Road and railroads were lacking.

General Alexander Samsonov was chosen to command the Russian Second Army. He was tasked with invading East Prussia. His blunders would lead to the disastrous Battle of Tannenberg which would set the tone for the rest of war. Russia began its offensive into East Prussia. The goal was to defeat the German army in East Prussia, and, after forcing them to retreat, to cut off the German Eighth Army as it tried to leave the region. The Russians had quick success.

However, the tables quickly turned. The German commanders chose a bold strategy: rather than continue to run before the Russians, the Germans moved straight against their foes, confronting Samsonov's forces even though the Russian forces were numerically superior. The Germans and Russians clashed in a bloody battle which would be known as the Battle of Tannenberg.

Key to the German success was their ability to decode the Russian communications. Although Russian leaders had known that the Germans were able to decode their messages, the Russians had continued to use old code. Additionally, difficulties in communication and supplying the army hampered the Russian mobility on the battlefield. By August 28 and 29, the Russians became encircled and lost many personnel as they tried to break through the German lines. The situation was so hopeless that Samsonov committed suicide.

The loss to the Russian forces was staggering: the Germans had captured 92,000 and killed or wounded about 78,000. Only about 10,000 personnel from the entire Russian Second Army escaped. The Russians also suffered devastating losses of materiel. On the opposing side, losses were less costly. Although over 150,000 Germans had participated in the battle, their forces had suffered only about 12,000 casualties. Although the Russian Second Army had been destroyed, the Germans were still aware that the Russian First Army was still an active force in the region. While the German victory at Tannenberg was key, it did not end the conflict.

The losses beginning early in the war took a toll on the country, as did the tsar's absence from the capital. While Tsar Nicholas spent time trying to monitor the war, Alexandra, his wife, wreaked havoc on domestic affairs through her relationship with the controversial figure of Rasputin, a man that the tsarina revered. She believed that Rasputin had a special relationship with God, and she credited Rasputin with improving her son's health. Alexei, the only son of Nicholas and Alexandra, was a hemophiliac. This disease made even minor injuries dangerous to his life.

Although Rasputin may have correctly predicted the dangers of going to war, his presence did not improve the domestic situation. Leaders faced dismissal if they dared to criticize Alexandra's holy man. Rasputin also butted heads with the Duma.

Russian losses continued on the warfront, while the Germans made large gains. In 1916, the Germans had managed to conquer all of Poland, and were approaching Moscow, coming to within two hundred miles of the city. Understandably, the morale of the soldiers was nonexistent, but working conditions away from the front were equally bad. Strikes and chaos continued away from the front lines. Alexandra undermined the stability by dismissing more leaders who were unfriendly to Rasputin. By the time the cold weather arrived in St. Petersburg in December 1916, the people faced the harsh Russian winter with little food and little fuel. A cold, starving population had little to lose when they considered how little they benefitted from the current regime.

Frustrated with the situation, Prince Yusipov assassinated Rasputin, hoping that the death of the mystic would free the tsar and tsarina to be more involved in the problems at hand, but by the beginning of 1917 all sides recognized that Tsar Nicholas was no longer in charge of his absolute monarchy. The situation of the populace in the capital city deteriorated further.

SECTION 2.2: FEBRUARY/MARCH REVOLUTION

The end had arrived for the Romanov dynasty. Between March 8 and 10, demonstrators demanding food clashed with authorities who could not tame the situation. The mob became more volatile, destroying police stations. The authorities turned to the capital's army garrison and troops were ordered to return the protesters to their homes. After some engagements that ended with soldiers firing on protesters, the soldiers lost any desire to commit more violence against the civilians. On March 11, the tsar determined to quell the situation by dissolving the Duma. The situation only worsened as the Russian army turned to the side of the demonstrators. Within days Tsar Nicholas abdicated the throne, and over three hundred years of Romanov rule ended. Under the Julian calendar, which Russia still used at the time, the tsar abdicated on March 2, 1917. The date under the Gregorian calendar (adopted by the nation in 1918) was March 15, 1917.

The March Revolution was spontaneous. No leader had taken the head of the protestors. They had self-organized in the face of a disengaged government that was not meeting their most basic needs. In the vacuum left by the abdication of Tsar Nicholas, the Russian Provisional Government, led by Prince Georgy Lvov, tried to get a hold on the chaotic situation. Additionally, the Petrograd Soviet, or Workers' Council, became a power vying to represent the interests of the working class. Many viewed the provisional government as a mere tool of the upper class, a tool that was still not interested in addressing and solving the problems of the poor that had spurred the Revolution to take place from the start.

SECTION 2.3: INTERIM

The provisional government and the Petrograd Soviet began an uneasy relationship. The Soviet did not have the experience or desire to run the government bureaucracy, and the provisional government did not have the support of the workers and military. In many ways, from the start, the provisional government understood its precarious position before the Soviet's popular support. The Petrograd Soviet had to formalize its own structure during this time. The Soviet garnered the support of the socialists and Mensheviks who opposed the interests held by those in the Provisional Government.

Vladimir Lenin seized the moment to return from exile in Switzerland. He arrived on the scene in April 1917. Lenin directly opposed any further involvement in the war and any support of the provisional government. His views were captured in the April Theses, which were Lenin's exposition on his views, published after his return from Switzerland. Lenin wanted to motivate his fellow Bolsheviks and exiles returning from abroad to take action to defeat the provisional government. In the Theses, Lenin clearly decried those who would support liberal ideals or the provisional government. He instead pushed for a government that would give power to the workers. He urged his Bolsheviks to implement and advocate for communist policies. Lenin also made calculated use of propaganda, trying to win over the hungry masses. His clear strategy would place his followers in a prime position in the coming days.

The turbulence that carried over into July 1917 is known as the July Days. Lenin fled the country temporarily when the provisional government issued a warrant for his arrest. Meanwhile, Lvov was replaced with Alexander Kerensky as the provisional government's prime minister—the key leader of the government. Even as the Bolsheviks and other groups worked against him, Kerensky tried to maintain the Russian presence in the war. His difficulties only increased as the populace continued to face struggles with meeting their basic needs.

When soldiers under the command of Aleksandr Krymov turned toward St. Petersburg, Kerensky faced a difficult choice: appeal to the more marginalized communists and socialists or face a military coup. The Bolsheviks, Mensheviks, and Socialist Revolutionaries intervened on behalf of Kerensky. Although a military coup did not take place, Kerensky lost credibility as a leader, and the Bolsheviks gained momentum. By the end of August, the Bolsheviks were gaining popularity and support for the Soviets in many major cities.

SECTION 2.4: BOLSHEVIK REVOLUTION

On October 23, 1917 under the old-style calendar (November 7, 1917 under the new-style calendar) the October Revolution fulfilled Lenin's vision spelled out in the April Theses. In a 10-2 vote, the Central Committee, the governing body of the Bolsheviks, voted to carry out its vision of an organized and aggressive uprising to overthrow the provisional government. Lenin's vision was not a gradual descent into communism but rather a violent sprint. Over the past months, Lenin had presided over a plan that called for the Bolsheviks to gradually infiltrate into the leadership of major cities.

A revolutionary military committee, part of the Petrograd Soviet, was created just to oversee the process. Leon Trotsky, who had been elected as the chairman of the Petrograd Soviet, was also an avid supporter of Lenin. Trotsky stood with Lenin opposing Grigory Zinoviev and Lev Kamenev. Zinoviev and Kamenev would represent the left-leaning position later when Lenin's successor would be chosen.

Together, Trotsky and Lenin became a powerful team to plan and carry out a violent overthrow of the provisional government. Trotsky's efficient organization of a de facto Bolshevik armed force would later be put to use as he would be key in organizing the Red Army—the Bolshevik's military forces. Trotsky was soon second only to Lenin in the Bolshevik power structure.

The Bolshevik Red Guards, under the command of the Military Revolutionary Committee controlled by Trotsky, began occupying government buildings two days after Lenin's declaration that it was time to begin the October Revolution. While this was happening, the military forces in the city began taking part with the Red Guards. The Winter Palace, the symbol of the old regime's authority, came under attack on October 26, 1917. At that point there were few forces left to defend the building. Nearly all of the provisional government's cabinet surrendered. Kerensky, the prime minister, managed to escape. The Soviet government would later capitalize on reenactments to portray the assault on the Winter Palace as much more dramatic. However, in reality, few, if any, of those charged with guarding the building deemed the cause worthy of their deaths.

A majority of the Second Congress of Soviets determined to ratify the overthrow of the provisional government. The Congress approved a resolution that empowered the Soviets, thus legitimizing the Revolution. These actions were not favored by all participants. The socialists and Mensheviks opposed the Revolution. They did not see it as a legitimate change of government. Those opposing the October 1917 Revolution walked out of the Congress and lost any opportunity to temper Bolshevik control.

On October 26, 1917, Bolsheviks were placed in the cabinet while the country awaited the election of the All-Russian Constituent Assembly. The Constituent Assembly was to be a democratically elected and constitutionally guided organization to govern the country. The Bolsheviks at first supported the idea of the Constituent Assembly running the nation. They allowed elections to take place on November 12, 1917. Lenin's followers gave lip-service to the authority of the Constituent Assembly that was slated to be the governing authority of the nation.

A majority, around 60% of the eligible population, turned out for the election. While the conditions for tallying the vote were not ideal, as the war and lack of communications kept the numbers from being timeously reported, the party with the largest number of votes, around 40%, was the Socialist Revolutionaries. The Bolsheviks received a much smaller portion of the vote—only about 24%. There was a clear divide between the rural and urban areas. The vast majority of voters in the rural areas supported the socialists, while the workers in the cities supported the well-organized Bolsheviks.

Of course, once Lenin surmised that the Bolshevik party would not carry a majority in the Constituent Assembly, his group began a campaign to discredit the democratically elected legislative body. Bolshevik leaders alerted their organizations, including military forces under their influence. They were prepared to take action against the Constituent Assembly should the Bolsheviks' interests be jeopardized. Lenin even published another "Theses" to unify the Bolshevik strategy concerning the Constituent Assembly. Lenin's clear message to followers was that the Constituent Assembly would have to be dismantled.

Following their leader's instruction, the Bolsheviks intimidated the legislative body. The Constituent Assembly met for a mere thirteen hours before the Bolsheviks succeeded in disbanding it. By January 18, 1918, the Bolsheviks had intimidated delegates to the point that they feared to take any action, including meeting for a second day. The legislative body had lasted from 4 p.m. on January 17 until 5 a.m. on January 18. The third Congress of Soviets, called together after the dissolution of the assembly, was mostly composed of Bolsheviks and the All-Russian Central Executive Committee, also ratified the action to disband the Constituent Assembly, trying to legitimize the Bolsheviks' actions.

The non-Bolshevik groups decided to try to reintegrate within the Soviet and, in part, they were successful. However, when they did win support, many times the Bolsheviks refused to recognize outcomes of elections that the Bolsheviks lost. Thus, even though other groups tried to exert influence over the government, they were systemically failing.

While the country struggled internally, the Bolsheviks took charge of settling some of the foreign affairs problems. The Bolsheviks signed the Treaty of Brest-Litovsk on March 3, 1918, in the city of the same name. Russia officially ended its involvement in World War I through this agreement with the Central Powers. The Treaty provided some respite for the Bolsheviks who were going to engage in a bloody civil war against the Mensheviks.

The terms of the treaty were not friendly to Russian geographical claims. It asserted that many areas that had once been part of the Russian Empire would be their own sovereign states. Finland, Estonia, Latvia, Ukraine, and Lithuania were endorsed as independent states. Not named among the independent states, Polish people rioted and any support felt for the Central Powers died. The result of the treaty was dramatic: Russia lost a quarter of the population that it had claimed under the Russian Empire. Russia also lost significant portions of its industry and 90% of its coal mines. Germany gained influence over all the independent states as it ensured that the states were ruled by German aristocracy. Germany was also able to transfer many of its battle-hardened soldiers to the Western Front.

In addition to the losses of territory to German influence, Russia lost lands that it had taken from the Ottoman Empire. The Turkish Grand Vizier (a post equivalent to prime minister), Talat Pasha, demanded the return of all territory that Russia had conquered during the Russo-Turkish War. Only parts of that land that had fallen under the control of the Democratic Republic of Georgia would be returned to the Soviet Union in March 1921, when the Soviets dominated Georgia. The territory that fell under the Democratic Republic of Armenia ended up under the control of Turkey.

SECTION 2.5: CIVIL WAR

The Bolshevik grip on power was at first a fragile one and was only affirmed after a bloody civil war. Over the course of the battle between the "White" and the "Red" Russians, over two million combatants would die, while about thirteen million civilians would perish.

In order to support their military effort, the Reds employed war communism, also known as military communism. This system was in place in territories controlled by the Soviets during the Russian Civil War and lasted from 1918 until 1921. The principles of the system involved extensive centralization. The Soviets took control of the industry and forced centralized management. Foreign trade was also centralized. The requisition of surplus agricultural products was centralized, leaving the peasants with barely enough food for their own subsistence. The Russian term for this was *Prodrazvyorstka* which meant *food apportionment*. Not just food, but most other items were rationed by a central authority. There was no tolerance for strikers anymore. The penalty for striking could be death, and discipline overall was very harsh. Those who were not part of the working class were forced into various types of manual labor. The government also centralized control of transportation assets like the railroads and forbade all private enterprise, as it would detract from resources that would support the war effort.

At heart, these practices tried to ensure that the cities and military would not be affected by the ongoing civil war. The Red Army needed food and weapons in a time when infrastructure was likely being destroyed by the other side in the conflict. These policies started in June 1918 and ended on March 21, 1921 when the New Economic Policy (NEP) appeared. The Supreme Economic Council, or Vesenkha, ensured that the war communism applied across all segments of the economy.

After the end of World War I, many of the allied nations sent troops to fight against the Bolshevik's Red Army, refusing to recognize the legitimacy of the new regime; however, by the summer of 1919, many of them withdrew as the Red Army gained momentum. The White Army suffered defeat after defeat as major campaigns faced stiff opposition by the Reds. The Red Army also faced pressure from Poland. Poland, eager to have a buffer between itself and Russia, initiated combat. The Poles wanted to create this space by carving Belorussia and Ukraine from the Soviet sphere of influence. The conflict began in April of 1920, but by the middle of the summer, the Poles were retreating before the Red Army. The Red Army nearly advanced into Warsaw; however, due to the Poles' tenacity and their ability to break the Red Army communication code, the Poles held, and a peace treaty was signed. The end of the conflict in Poland, and the Red Army's alliance with the Ukrainian Black Army, were critical in the fall of 1920. The White Army was defeated.

As hostilities ceased, the Bolsheviks could focus on internal policies, especially because any tsarist claim to power ended with the murder of Tsar Nicholas and his family in July of 1918. Lenin would experiment with economic policies to revive the war-torn country, and he would take measures to secure his own authority.

The concept of secret police existed in Russia before the Soviet Union. Different security units were created under the tsars to guard against the constant threat of assassination that existed after the mid-1800s. However, Lenin's new regime and all future Soviet leaders would adopt similar tactics, and the secret police were a storied threat to the Russian people beginning shortly after the October Revolution. The secret police would be known by different names through the course of the Soviet Union's history: Cheka, OGPU, NKVD, NKGB. However, its function remained the same. It used harsh measures to eliminate any opposition to the ruling power. Individuals had no rights with which to oppose the secret police, and the force administered summary justice, whether that was torture, exile, or execution.

SECTION 2.6: NEW ECONOMIC POLICY (NEP)

From 1921 until 1928, the Russian economy operated under the NEP. Lenin had determined to change the economic policy in order to bolster the faltering economy that had suffered during the world war, revolution, and civil war. The NEP did permit some private businesses. Small enterprises could exist; however, there was state control of all major industries, including the banking industry, manufacturing, and foreign trade. Farmers also saw the forced requisition of their produce diminish. On March 21, 1921, during its 10th Congress, the All-Russian Communist Party decreed that farmers owed a specific tax, namely, all products in excess of what they themselves needed to survive. The government would use a similar approach in industry as well, meaning that the workers or producers would be left with little of the fruits of their labor.

During the time of the NEP, the Soviet Union faced a halving of the urban population. This was concerning to the leaders of the USSR. The urban population had been in the revolution, and composed the demographic that supported the communist party most adamantly. With their power base dwindling, leaders feared that they could lose control of the entire country.

Meanwhile, there were also concrete disadvantages to the NEP. The rural areas enjoyed free market influences such that the grain production dramatically increased, driving the price of grain down. However, government centralization of industry slowed the production of consumer goods down, causing the price of goods to increase. The cost increase for items would spur farmers to hold on to their excess grain, later making them the target of suspicion. The falling cost of grain contrasted with the rising cost of items was termed the scissor effect.

 Section 3: Pre-War Stalinism

SECTION 3.1: LENIN'S SUCCESSOR

Lenin lived only a few years after the Soviet Union won the civil war, and there would be a fierce power struggle to determine who would fill the leadership position when Lenin died. Lenin anticipated his own death and tried to influence who would be chosen as his successor. In the last months of his life, Lenin wrote a document that was to guide the communist party in choosing a leader. This document became known as Lenin's Testament. Written between the end of 1922 and the first weeks of 1923, Lenin expounded on a vision to change the structure of the government. The Testament also critiqued different leaders of the Soviet Union, and it suggested that one, Joseph Stalin, be removed. At that time Stalin was the General Secretary of the Soviet Communist Party's Central Committee. Stalin had been a staunch supporter of Lenin in the years leading up to Lenin's death; however, Lenin had come to mistrust Stalin, an ethnic Georgian, who wielded tremendous power in his position as General Secretary.

Lenin intended his Testament to reach the ears of the Twelfth Party Congress of the Communist Party by the time of their meeting in April 1923. His worsening health prevented that. When Lenin suffered his third stroke in March 1923, he suffered paralysis and an inability to speak. Lenin's wife, Nadezhda Krupskaya, did not permit the Testament to be released. She was hoping that her husband would recover. He never did. Lenin died on January 21, 1924, and afterwards Krupskaya relinquished the Testament to the Communist Party's Central Committee Secretariat to be given to the Thirteenth Party Congress set to meet in May 1924.

The revelation of the Testament came as a shock to Stalin. He had styled himself as an ardent supporter of Lenin. Stalin reacted to the Testament by offering to resign from his position. Other leaders saw his offer as an act of humility, and Stalin was allowed to keep his position.

Stalin began maneuvering for the highest level of authority possible. The political landscape became divided into two groups: the leftists, consisting of Zinoviev, Kamenev, and Trotsky, and the rightest, consisting of Nikolai Bukharin, Alexei Rykov, and Mikhail Tomsky, all of whom supported Stalin. Bukharin was a powerful figure, but eventually all who opposed Stalin were marginalized as he secured his authority and became Lenin's successor.

SECTION 3.2: COLLECTIVIZATION

By the end of the 1920s, Russia was still underdeveloped by western standards. The Soviet Union also feared for its security with the rising threats of Japan, France, and Great Britain. There was also a push for the government to make more progress in achieving socialist policies. Although the NEP had been in place for several years, the true Bolsheviks wanted to take a dramatic step away from any vestige of the free market system. Some business people had managed to prosper under the NEP and stood out from the workers. Grain production had also fallen, and providing basic subsistence was still an issue. By 1926, Stalin opposed the NEP and was on the verge of taking dramatic action. In 1927, grain production was down by at least 30%. Stalin changed his position to one that dramatically opposed the NEP. As Stalin became more and more critical of the NEP, his opinions were even farther to the left than those of leaders like Trotsky and Zinoviev.

Late in 1927, Stalin crystallized his vision for the nation's economy. The nation's domestic affairs would be reordered by the first of Stalin's five-year plans. The five-year plans became notorious as the central government would hand down its plan for economic development. The plans delivered ambitious goals that would often force changes without any thought for the collateral damage that might be inflicted on the nation.

In 1928, the communist party endorsed Stalin's first five-year plan. The plan had two main prongs: collectivization and industrialization. Stalin's desire was that through his plans, he could expunge all traces of capitalism that had existed under the more liberal NEP. The Soviet Union was to become an embodiment of socialist ideals, without any regard to the harm that it would inflict on millions of individuals.

The year 1928 became a pivotal moment. At the beginning of the year, Stalin went to Novosibirsk. As he visited rural areas, he accused farmers of hiding their grain production. He ordered the arrests of the farmers and the confiscation of their crops. Stalin took the grain back to Moscow. His actions were merely the precursor to a mass seizure of crops. Stalin endorsed groups who went to the farmers and requisitioned the crops. The farmers and these procurement squads clashed violently. Stalin commanded these actions and encouraged harsh measures to force the peasants to give up the fruits of their labor.

Leaders in the Central Committee, including Bukharin, criticized both the new policies and the fact that Stalin had taken unilateral action without their knowledge. However, a course was set to further punish the kulak class. The kulaks were the Russian peasant class that had appeared after the serfs were freed in the 1800s. This class of peasant farmer had enough success to be able to expand their agriculture, own their own farm, and employ others to work on the farm. As this group became Stalin's target, they opposed Stalin's new policy even to the point of violent resistance. However, the resistance was fruitless. The Politburo endorsed Stalin's new vision to collectivize the nation's agriculture and put an end to the kulak class. In 1930, the Politburo voted on a proposal that would intentionally take all property from the kulaks and destroy them as a class of people. The communist party saw this as a way to gain the support of the larger masses of peasants who were suffering from famine.

This process became known as dekulakization. As Stalin carried this process out, millions of kulaks faced repression. Although estimates vary, the direct and collateral effects of this new policy was the death of millions. Millions of kulaks were directly impacted by execution, arrest, and exile to less favorable circumstances. Those that were not overtly executed by Stalin's forces faced deadly conditions in Stalin's growing work camp system. The camp system became known as the Gulag. The purpose of the camps was two-fold: to get cheap labor and to punish opponents of the regime. Stalin referred to this forced labor as *socially useful work*.

Simultaneously, while Stalin was purging the country of the kulaks, he was replacing the old system through collectivization. Stalin began formulating five-year plans to direct the economy. As a part of the first five-year plan, Stalin mandated that individuals would no longer control their own farming efforts. In the 1920s, communes began to arise. These communes that resembled earlier collective farming associations became known as *kolkhozy*. Instead, the land was given over to collectives. Collective farming described the land being taken from the control of individuals and given to groups. The group was supposed to work the land together either under direct control of the state or at the direction of the cooperative's leadership.

The Russian peasants paid the price for collectivization. The government gave them even less in return for the crops that they produced. The number of livestock and the production of food dropped sharply. To illustrate the damage done to the country by collectivization, the Soviet Union did not return to the numbers of livestock that it had in 1928 until the late 1950s. The immediate result of collectivization in Russia through the mid-1930s was hunger for large swathes of the population and the death of up to ten million kulaks.

While Stalin was formulating his plan to reorganize Russian agriculture, the rest of the world was considering how to prevent another world war. Signed in 1928, the Kellogg-Briand Pact, or Pact of Paris as it was also known, was a treaty among many nations, including the Soviet Union. The treaty took its name from the U.S. Secretary of State, Frank B. Kellogg, and the French foreign minister, Aristide Briand. The treaty tried to outlaw war as a tool of foreign policy. It did allow for war as necessary for self-defense. The Americans, desiring to prevent entanglement in European rivalries, originally only contemplated a treaty between France and the U.S. Kellogg expanded the treaty so as to preserve his nation's range of options, suggesting that the treaty include every nation. Formally called the General Treaty for the Renunciation of War, the treaty would not be successful at preventing all conflict. However, it did usher in an era of nations trying to find better legal justifications for aggression. Another effect was that many times nations simply did not declare war when launching hostilities.

SECTION 3.3: INDUSTRIALIZATION

Alongside his new agricultural policy, Stalin also wanted to drive the nation forward in industrial development. Stalin was concerned with the growth of the nation's heavy industry. Stalin's five-year plan set forth unrealistic and specific quotas that industry had to meet. Alongside these quotas, Stalin mandated centralization of all industries and services. His plan spurred a flurry of construction, with new plants appearing in cities that Stalin directed would become industrial centers. Much of Stalin's impetus in industrialization was motivated by his fear of potential armed conflict with other more industrialized nations in the west.

While the activity in these sectors did increase, the actual output could not meet the impossible quotas that were set by central authorities. On top of the impossible production goals, the centralized direction of the economy did not take into consideration the true needs of the people. Shortages of commonly needed domestic products became normal. These shortages included food. Social changes were required as well to make the 350% increase in production occur. Under centralized direction, the first five-year plan saw the numbers of industrial workers nearly double to over six million workers in 1932. One outgrowth of the five-year plan was a growth in the use of forced labor as a means to provide a workforce for the industrialization. Those convicted of even minor infractions might find themselves a part of the forced labor in the Russian work camps.

World powers noticed the growth taking place in the nation. Due in large part to new media coverage of the Russian economic changes, nations like the United States of America recognized the Soviet Union as an official nation. The other positive effect of the five-year plan would be felt later in the next world war when Stalin would need his industry to counter the German army. The five-year plan had many failures as well. The workers were demoralized by impossible quotas and millions died as a direct and indirect result of the plan.

The second five-year plan began in 1933. Stalin formulated the plan in 1932 with an official start date in 1933. Key parts of this plan involved an emphasis on heavy industry. Steel production was especially important, and as a result of the second five-year plan, Russia became a steel-producing powerhouse, not far behind other industrialized nations such as Germany. The plan also resulted in gains in communications and transportation. The plan also motivated large cultural shifts. Childcare was introduced as a means to expand the working class as mothers could enter the workforce. Stalin also implemented measures in the second five-year plan aimed at entirely eradicating religion through closing churches and eliminating religious leaders. In the third five-year plan, which would carry the Soviet Union into the Second World War, Stalin oversaw a rise in the production of armaments. The third five-year plan lasted from 1938 until 1941.

An important movement that sprung from the second five-year plan was the Stakhanovite movement. The movement took its name from a worker, Aleksei Stakhanov, who had worked to meet and exceed his quota for coal mining. Soon Stakhanov became the symbol of the communist party's idealized worker who not only met, but exceeded their quota. Competitions lauding productivity as well as awards were named after the coal miner. The government gave the Stakhanovite movement's highly motivated workers credit for dramatically improving productivity across the entire country.

SECTION 3.4: REIGN OF TERROR

Leading up to 1936, great tension existed between a desire for rights for the individual Russian and Stalin's desire to consolidate his own power. In 1933, Stalin had implemented policies designed to relieve the situation in overcrowded prisons. He had ordered the release of those in prison who had committed minor offenses, and he momentarily halted mass arrests. Additionally, in September 1934, Stalin acted to create a Politburo commission that would examine whether individuals were being rightly imprisoned.

In 1936, the Soviet Union adopted a constitution. This constitution, officially ratified on December 5, 1936, protected individual rights. While the constitution would be known as the Stalin Constitution, thanks to Stalin's propaganda machine, the constitution was not authored by Stalin. A commission including prominent leaders such as Nikolai Bukharin, Karl Radek, and Yakovlev had designed the document. These notable leaders would later be executed during Stalin's purges.

The constitution was meant to provide more rights to the individual citizen. These rights included giving all citizens the right to vote. It also recognized a myriad of other rights for the Russian citizen that were designed to provide security to the Russian individual over the course of their life. These rights included social welfare programs such as health care, housing, work, care for sick or aging workers, and education. Notably, the constitution attempted to reorganize the Russian government through directed elections. The new government was to be made up of directly elected bodies. Ironically, although Stalin had little to do with the authorship of the new constitution, he would benefit from the constitution in two ways. Firstly, other nations gave him credit for the document, which many nations hailed as embodying democratic ideals. Secondly, the new organization of the government acted to consolidate Stalin's grasp on power. Thus, the constitution cemented external support for and internal control by Stalin.

At the same time, concerns over national security and Sergey Kirov's murder also shaped Stalin's course. After Kirov, a prominent member of the communist party, was killed, Stalin assessed his own vulnerability. He began improving his own security forces and avoiding public appearances. Slowly, state sponsored repression grew. Stalin empowered the NKVD, the name of the secret police at that time, to make determinations that did not involve any sort of court involvement. There were no due process rights for those individuals targeted by the secret police.

These incremental moves led to a dark time in Russian history that would be known as the Great Purge. The Great Purge was a systematic drive by Stalin to consolidate his power and implement true socialism through persecution and repression. The Great Purge would last for two years, from 1936 until 1938, but its effects would be felt for decades. Stalin engineered accusations against ranking communist party members, alleging that individuals did not support the communist party and were actually subversives employed by western capitalist powers. Those accused faced imprisonment and exile.

Stalin targeted many groups in his bid to consolidate power. Members of the communist party and government employees were especially targeted. These people were accused of being counter-revolutionaries. Peasants, a class of people that faced Stalin's ire because he accused them of chronically withholding their crops, also faced widespread repression. The leadership of the Red Army was also suspect and faced Stalin's oppression. All individuals feared the secret police, and there was a universal fear of incarceration, exile, and execution.

The fear of the Russian secret police was such that the worst period of the Great Purge takes its name from Nikolai Yezhov, who headed the secret police during that time. The most severe period of purges taking place between 1937 and 1938 is called Yezhovshchina—literally meaning the times or doings of Yehzov.

Stalin orchestrated trials, known as the Moscow Trials, to publicly eliminate his political opposition. A total of three trials took place between 1936 and 1938, alleging that senior leaders in the nation were either actively helping other nations by sabotaging Russia or that senior leaders were counter-revolutionaries. The drama unfolding at the trials was nearly incomprehensible to international spectators. Leaders who had been devoted followers of Lenin proclaimed that they had committed unbelievable offenses and that they should be executed.

In August 1936, the notable party members Grigory Zinoviev and Lev Kamenev were among 16 defendants at the first Moscow Trial. The defendants faced a multitude of outrageous charges. Included among the charges were allegations that the defendants had murdered Sergey Kirov and planned to assassinate Stalin. After implausible confessions from all defendants, the court issued and carried out death sentences. The second Moscow Trial took place early in 1937 and involved the same script. Defendants were accused of committing offenses designed to undermine the revolution and the nation. After confessions and sentencing, the defendants were either executed or sent to labor camps, which resulted in death as well.

Some observers asserted that the proceedings were fair. Observers who watched the defendants confess in open court did not perceive any signs of torture or maltreatment. However, time would show that the defendants had been the victims of various forms of torture resulting in their eventual confessions.

During the second trial, one of the defendant's confessions referred to an organized movement of Trotsky's followers. Stalin used this confession to justify a third trial. In March 1928, the last and most famous of the Moscow Trials took place. Known as the Trial of Twenty-One, the defendants even included a former head of the NKVD, showing that no one was off-limits from Stalin's purges. Observers could no longer believe that there was any veil of legality to the trials. Bukharin, respected as a true adherent to Marxism, was tried and executed despite his loyalty to socialist ideals. While many members of the regime dragged their feet at trying their comrade Bukharin, Stalin expedited the process by replacing the then-head of the NKVD with Nikolai Yezhov. While the purges of the Red Army were not as public, Stalin removed the majority of high-ranking officers, and close to 8% of the total officer corps. Many of the lower level officers were returned to service as the exigencies of the world war brought about a reconsideration of their status.

Although the purge of leadership received attention, any group could fall under Stalin's suspicion and criticism. Writers, artists, and even astronomers faced persecution by Stalin. Various ethnic groups or those who owned their own businesses also faced the purges. Even those communists who had immigrated to Russia to live in the cradle of socialist ideals faced widespread persecution and execution.

Sometimes people were arrested just to fulfill quotas. Stalin might call for a number of people to be arrested, and much of this helped to fill labor camps that would carry out Stalin's pet projects such as the building of canals, where forced labor would have to dig through the tundra with sticks or their bare hands. To meet their numbers, authorities might sweep through areas where marginalized individuals would gather and arrest the number needed. There were even quotas for confessions.

The targets of Stalin's persecution faced arrest, torture, exile, execution, or murder without any legal recourse. In the process of being forced to confess their own wrongdoing, these individuals were often pressured to name others who were committing these "crimes" of being counter-revolutionaries or saboteurs working for foreign governments.

Once the arrest and confession occurred, the secret police *troikas*, or *group of three people*, would determine the sentence to be enforced. These sentences of either exile or death were rapid and unquestioned.

SECTION 3.5: CULTURE

Stalin's control over the Russian nation enabled him to shape Russian culture. Through his control of all social institutions, including the media and the educational system, Stalin encouraged a personality culture that lauded him as a new father of all Russians. Just as Russians at different times in the nation's history had viewed the tsar as the "Little Father," a benevolent figure who was interested in the well-being of the common individual, Stalin utilized his propaganda machine to propagate a similar view of himself among his citizens. In essence, Stalin hoped to replace traditional religion with a glorified version of himself as a leader.

Stalin introduced social institutions or manipulated them to empower him. While women had temporarily enjoyed more liberal views on marriage, divorce, and procreation under Lenin, Stalin favored a return to more traditional views, including a state-led emphasis on marriage and family. This could have been in response to a crisis of homeless children that grew at the beginning of the 1930s.

While the personality cult of Stalin grew and Russian society returned to a more traditional nuclear model, Stalin determined to develop a socialist version of fine arts that had once flourished in the nation. In place of an emphasis on creativity, the new socialist fine arts placed an emphasis on communicating the ideals and goals of socialism and communism. At its core, socialist realism, not to be confused with social realism, a different type of art, was a tool for propaganda. This style of art would be honed under the Soviet Union but would be adopted by other communist countries. Unlike social realism, which tried to portray the plight of the poor in a realistic manner, socialist realism was meant to glorify the working-class proletariat through realistic images. This style appeared in all art forms.

The government itself set out guidelines for artistic work in 1934. The work had to meet four requirements. All art had to be proletariat-centric, relevant, and easily understood by the workers. Art needed to be typical, meaning that the subject matter of the artwork had to be everyday subjects. Art had to be realistic, prohibiting romanticism or abstraction in form. Lastly, and perhaps most importantly, art had to be partisan, supporting the ideals of the communist party.

Cultural policy would also be strongly influenced by the ideas of Andrei Zhdanov. Zhdanov became the director of cultural policy in 1946 and would immediately take action to censor artists. His name became the title of soviet cultural norms known as Zhdanovism. Zhdanovism held that the creative forces within the Soviet Union expressed through the different genres of literature and fine arts had to comply with the communist party's ideology. If an artist dared to oppose the ruling party, they faced repression and censure. The policy was only reversed in 1952 when leaders acknowledged that the policy had a detrimental effect on artistic work.

Socialist realism appeared in the productions of Sergei Eisenstein, Russia's most famous film director during the early years of the Soviet Union. In the 1920s, Eisenstein produced revolutionary masterpieces like *The Battleship Potemkin* and *Ten Days That Shook the World*, and epics focusing on historical Russian figures, including his masterpiece *Ivan the Terrible*. Eisenstein also forayed into the western film industry unsuccessfully and faced the establishment's suspicion when he returned in the early 1930s. Eisenstein avoiding Stalin's ire by producing the film *Alexander Nevsky* that would be heavily utilized as an anti-German propaganda tool. Key among Eisenstein's techniques was the interspersing of traditional Russian quotes with quotes from the revolution's leader, Lenin.

Vsevolod Emilevich Meyerhold was another who helped to establish socialist realism. He was a theater director and producer who experimented with unconventional settings that would be influential. Joining the revolution in 1917, he headed the theater portion of the party's education commissariat by 1920. His important works included an initial production of *Mystery-Bouffe* in 1918, a play by Vladimir Mayakovsky that celebrated the triumph of the proletariat over the bourgeoisie. Meyerhold experimented with different theories in his productions, including constructionism. His constructivist works included *The Magnificent Cuckold*, written by Fernand Crommelynck and *The Death of Tarelkin* by Alexander Sukhovo-Kobylin. Meyerhold eventually faced suspicion, criticism, and execution at the hands of the establishment.

On the literary front, Maxim Gorky became the author who established the standard for Soviet revolutionary literature and socialist realism. The name was actually the pseudonym for Alexei Peshkov and meant Maxim the Bitter. *The Mother*, written by Gorky in 1906, was known as the seminal work of socialist realism. This book models the guidelines set by the communist party later in the 1930s. Using a realistic setting for the Russian individual—a female factory-worker who is struggling with poverty and starvation on a daily basis—the ideals of the party are lauded as she empowers herself through her son's revolutionary instruction.

In the genre of poetry, the writing of Anna Akhmatova stands out during this time period. Anna Gorenko used the pen name of Anna Akhmatova as she created art that would have a lasting influence on Russian poetry. She produced both shorter and longer pieces and covered many topics that were central to her time. Her poetry topics included the treatment of artistic women, time, memory, and the dangerous times of the purges. Her larger work *Requiem* addressed the Great Purge and Stalin's reign of terror. Her work faced criticism and censure. Eventually her poems were banned even though she was nominated for a Nobel Prize in the 1960s.

SECTION 3.6: NATIONALITIES

Although Stalin was not an ethnic Russian, he created a policy that would serve to consolidate his power through the repression of nationalities under the Soviet Union. While emphasizing the twin values of centralism and conformity, Stalin determined that he could better consolidate his power through the assimilation of other nations more effectively into Russian culture. Stalin had a vision for a united Soviet people that would be able to overthrow the capitalist west. The Russian language and culture were Stalin's vehicle to accomplish these visions. To this end, Stalin mandated instruction in Russian language. He also weakened all satellite governments and strengthened Moscow's control. Along with these changes, overt persecution of other nationalists took place. Viewing those with nationalist ambitions as traitors, Stalin undermined regionalism through intentional starvation, the most dramatic example occurring in Ukraine, and resettlement.

Section 4: The Second World War

SECTION 4.1: PRE-WAR FOREIGN RELATIONS

While Russia underwent the purges of Stalin in the 1930s, its internal crisis would be dwarfed by the external threats during World War II. Although Stalin was responsible for the death of millions of Russians before the war, roughly 24 to 27 million Russians would die as a result of World War II. Of those millions of deaths, about 11 million would be soldiers either killed or missing from combat operations. The situation was so dire that around 800,000 women served in combat, exposing themselves to the front line just as their male counterparts did. The Russian civilians bore losses from intentional violence or indirect means such as starvation, exposure, or forced labor. This traumatic loss of life added to Stalin's propaganda machine and resulted in the war commonly being called the Great Patriotic War by the average Russian. While most Russians were unaware of the role that their own government played in the Nazi aggression, they were all too aware of the price that they paid for their victory.

Stalin had always been wary of other foreign powers before World War II. The Soviet Union was a signatory to the Kellogg-Briand Pact, but Stalin had also been motivated by keen realism to develop industrial capabilities, looking at the possibility of future armament against external threats. Stalin used the party narrative to his benefit. The condemnation of capitalism justified Russian isolationism and the idea that the western nations were only looking for an opportunity to attack the Soviet Union.

Ironically, it was the Soviet Union's meddling in foreign affairs that helped secure Hitler's rise to power. Stalin mandated that the communists in his sphere of influence would aid the National Socialist German Workers' Party, now famously known as the Nazi party, in an attempt to undermine the more moderate socialists. It was Stalin's dream that a Nazi party rise to power would bring about a communist revolution.

Stalin soon recognized the error of his ways. Between the years of 1934 to 1937, Russia attempted to mitigate the Nazi threat. Russia built relationships with Nazi opponents, including coalitions with more liberal communists. The Soviet Union also joined the fledgling League of Nations where it advocated against the threats of the National Socialist Party.

The Soviet Union built alliances with France and Czechoslovakia. Significantly, the Soviet Union sided with the Spanish Republicans during the Spanish Civil War. During the Spanish Civil War, the Russians provided a variety of support to the Republicans. Most of the support was in the form of equipment. The Soviet Union provided artillery, tanks, and planes to the Republicans in large numbers. While the League of Nations imposed an arms embargo, the Soviet Union ignored prohibitions and secretly gave weapons to the Republicans when no other power dared to. Germany and Italy provided arms to the other side in open defiance of the non-intervention agreement that prohibited international meddling in the supposedly Spain-internal conflict.

Stalin did approve a new unit of the Soviet Army, Section X, to aid the Republicans in an operation with the same name as the unit, Operation X. This new unit did not effectively aid the Republicans, as Stalin's cautious approach in supporting the Republicans meant that the weapons committed to the conflict were highly inferior to those contributed to the fascist side. Stalin pulled weapons from museums, captured stockpiles, and distant conflicts. However, he did send some modern tanks and fighter planes. Stalin also took great pains to camouflage the transportation of these goods, but the communication and transportation issues ensured that the Republicans received far fewer weapons than they needed. As the war did not favor the Republicans, by the end of 1938 Stalin ordered the withdrawal of Soviet assets. It was a propaganda tool for the fascists when Republican payments for Soviet armaments came to light. The Republic had paid for weapons from official gold reserves, using over two-thirds of those reserves during the course of the conflict.

Russia had also provided help in the form of military advisors. As many as 3,000 Soviets acted in this capacity. Many of the tanks and planes were operated directly by a scant 700-member force of Soviet volunteers. Significantly, the Soviet Union used its influence over communist parties across the globe to recruit members who formed "International Brigades." The Russian secret police were also involved in operations. The NKVD carried out acts to influence the Republican government. Foreigners like Vittorio Vidali, Iosif Grigulevich and, Alexander Orlov carried out Russian-style purges of Spanish Nationalists, Catholics, anarchists, and even other Marxists like Andreu Nin and José Robles.

While the fascists gained the upper hand in Spain, European powers appeased Hitler's increasing demands. As Stalin observed the French and British acquiescence to German demands on Czech territory at Munich in 1938, he realized he could not hope for an alliance with those nations to defeat Hitler. Stalin was determined to take a different approach.

In May 1939, Stalin strategically replaced Maksim Litvinov, a Jew, with Vyacheslav Molotov. Molotov began secretly negotiating with Germany's foreign minister, Joachim von Ribbentrop. Although the result of these negotiations would be formally known as the Treaty of Non-Aggression between Germany and the Soviet Union, the agreement would be informally known as the Molotov-Ribbentrop Pact. Dated August 23, 1939, and signed early in the morning of August 24, 1939, the agreement detailed a new, uneasy alliance between Germany and the Soviet Union. The agreement pledged that the two nations would not take action against each other and that if a third party attacked either of the nations, the non-attacked nation would remain neutral. The agreement would survive until Germany initiated Operation Barbarossa on June 22, 1941, which signaled the invasion of German troops into Russian territory.

The agreement also carved out areas of influence in Europe, assigning Germany and Russia specific lands that they could each expect to control in the case of a conflict that would disrupt the current sovereign states. This agreement was the precursor to the invasions of Poland by both Russia and Germany so that the two nations divided Polish territory as set forth in the Molotov-Ribbentrop Pact. The Soviets also looked to expand on their assigned territories by assuming control of Finnish territory, and swallowing up the nations of Estonia, Latvia, Lithuania, and sections of Romania. Meanwhile, on

September 1, 1939, Germany attacked Poland. World War II officially began as France and Britain declared war on Germany two days later.

The Winter War was the name given to the conflict between the Soviet Union and Finland during the winter of 1939 into 1940. The conflict was short, ending in March, 1940. The Moscow Peace Treaty ended the conflict but doomed Finland to serious losses. The Soviet Union seized over 10% of the Finnish pre-war territory. Significantly, the agreement stripped Finland of 30% of its assets. However, the results were not as significant as the Soviet Union had hoped. The Soviets had desired a complete conquest of Finland and the annexation of the entire country. The Finns survived the conflict with their sovereignty intact. The conflict was not popular in the international community, and the Soviets faced losses not only of reputation but also in personnel. However, the Soviet Union's territorial gains along the edge of Lake Ladoga, directly beside Leningrad, would be crucial in the upcoming world war.

SECTION 4.2: THE COURSE OF THE WAR

Operation Barbarossa marked the beginning of German aggression against Russia and Russia's involvement in World War II on June 22, 1941. The scale of the attack was massive. The Axis powers fielded more than four million troops over a front that stretched for more than 1,800 miles. The operation has the dubious distinction of being the largest offensive that the world has ever seen. Alongside the soldiers, 600,000 vehicles and 750,000 horses were used to transport the forces. Not only was the operation significant for its size, it would also produce the largest number of casualties ever seen by a conflict in world history. Everything about the operation was superlative: the most soldiers, the largest battles, the most casualties, the worst atrocities, and indescribable conditions on both sides.

The planning for the operation had started more than six months before, on December 18, 1941, and the operation would last for nearly a year. The eventual effects of the conflict would seal the fate of Hitler's regime. Before Operation Barbarossa, the German potential for war gains was unlimited, but afterwards it was clear that the German industrial machine was not invincible. As Operation Barbarossa ground to a halt, Hitler demanded successes which committed the Germans to a series of grueling battles and spelled Germany's eventual defeat. The major German operations, including the Siege of Leningrad, Operation Nordlicht, and the Battle of Stalingrad, would slowly sap the German strength.

At the outset of the operation, the Germans had decided on a three-pronged attack on Russia. First, Army Group North had orders to sweep through the Baltic region and capture the former capital of the Tsarist Russia, now renamed Leningrad. In the middle, Army Group Center was tasked with capturing first Smolensk and then defeating the Soviet capital, Moscow. Army Group South was to advance through the fertile agricultural regions. It was ordered to capture Kiev and then move toward the Caucasus, where the Germans could seize strategic oil fields.

Upon the German invasion of Russia, Stalin took on the title of Marshal of the Soviet Union, in essence the commander in chief of the Russian military. Georgy Zhukov was put in the position of the highest ranking military leader in the Soviet Union. Zhukov would achieve fame as Russia's brilliant and potentially greatest military leader. Stalin also took measures to prevent threats from ethnically German peoples living in Russia. From 1941 until 1943, Stalin exiled large populations of Volgans and Tatars to his Gulag, fearing they would have much in common with the German invaders.

The first three weeks of Operation Barbarossa resulted in massive losses to the Russians, losses in both personnel of over 750,000 soldiers and materiel. Reacting to the losses, Stalin seized even more power within the government, taking absolute authority over the country's war while Germany inflicted ghastly losses on the Russian Army. By the end of 1941, the German Army had killed millions of Russian soldiers. However, Hitler was unable to secure a decisive victory over the Soviet Union. The Russians were hanging on even though the Germans had overrun large portions of Russian territory, including important gains of land that the Russians desperately needed. The Germans controlled Ukraine, which was of great economic importance to the Russians. However, the Germans had been unable to reach Moscow, and the Germans would never have the strength to mount an organized, powerful operation like Barbarossa again.

The Battle of Leningrad would be an important victory for the Russians. In the spring of 1941, the Germans began their attack against the city. The Germans saw Leningrad as a key conquest in the overall subjugation of Russia. The Russians mounted a desperate defense of the city. In positions that stretched over nearly 300 miles, over 500,000 Russians fought for their city. The Germans moved into the suburbs of the city before their offensive lost momentum. The city was under siege when all roads into the city were severed by the German advance on September 8, 1941. As with many other events along the front, this siege, which lasted until January 27, 1944, is likely the longest and costliest siege in world history. The siege officially lasted 872 days.

During the first part of the Battle of Leningrad, from July until September 1941, the Germans had successfully routed Russian forces throughout the Baltics. The Russians struggled to hold the Germans in the face of superior technology; however, the prospect of losing such a symbolic stronghold weighed heavily on the Russian forces. The Russians hung on, fighting through the loss of significant lines of transportation. On August 30, 1941, the Germans successfully took railroad lines, denying the city important resources of food, materiel, and soldiers. After September 8, 1941, Leningrad was only able to receive supplies from air drops or lake crossings. Neither of these options provided a means by which the city could receive sufficient supplies.

Over the course of the siege, over 641,000 people died of starvation alone. The situation looked dire in Leningrad as there was not sufficient food and supply stores to contemplate an offensive that could break the siege. However, as Russia was able to mount its operations to challenge the Germans at Stalingrad, the Germans could not simultaneously organize the final offensive that would be needed to completely defeat Leningrad. The defense of Leningrad would be one of the most draining portions of the entire war for the Soviets, but it was an important victory for the morale of the Russian people, who unified against the German threat.

Some relief came to the beleaguered city during the winter of 1942. During that time, the surface of the lake froze, and Russians were able to send trainloads of supplies into the city and transport loads of civilian refugees out. Over half a million people fled the city. The improved situation in the city, along with the Soviet success in Stalingrad, helped the Russian forces to break out of the siege and begin pushing the German forces back.

The battles at Kursk, Stalingrad, and Smolensk completely changed the momentum of the conflict, and Russian forces launched offensives to push the Germans out of their country.

Of all the important battles in Europe during World War II, the Battle of Stalingrad is likely the one that represents the turning point in the war against the Nazis. The German army would expend so many resources and so much time at Stalingrad that they could never recover. The defeat at Stalingrad pushed the Germans into obvious retreat, and spared Leningrad from a fatal offensive.

The Battle of Moscow was launched on October 2, 1941 under the codename Operation Typhoon. The Germans clearly recognized the strategic and symbolic importance of capturing the Soviet capital, and they deemed it as a measure of the success of Operation Barbarossa. Hitler counted on the capture of the city to end all Russian resistance and demoralize the Russian people. As the German advance slowed and failed to take the city, Hitler relieved the commander in chief, Walther von Brauchitsch. In a move that would be criticized by military experts and historians after the war, Hitler assumed command of the Wehrmacht. Not only did this subject the army to Hitler's ineptitude, but it also had the effect of distancing the leader from the officers most able to make sound tactical decisions. As the distance between Hitler and his most experienced officer corps grew, Hitler surrounded himself with inexperienced staff officers. The relationship between Hitler and his most combat-effective commanders would never recover, and Germany would pay a high price for the degraded performance of the Wehrmacht.

Where Germany had excelled at the lightning speed of its early war efforts—its blitzkrieg—it was not equipped for a war of attrition that would tax its resources on every side. The battle for Moscow was by no means a stinging defeat, but it would stop the German blitzkrieg that had assumed the war on the eastern front would end quickly and in favor of the Axis powers.

Stalin gambled on Hitler sustaining efforts against Moscow and transferred forces to defend the capital from areas that were within striking distance of Japan. December saw the German forces a mere sixteen miles from the center of the Russian government, the Kremlin. Russian forces rallied, launching a counteroffensive on December 5, 1941. For the first time since the initiation of Operation Barbarossa, the Germans fell back, and the Russians were able to put fifty miles between the Kremlin and the Germans.

Stalin hoped to capitalize on this success and launch further offensives. Stalin announced plans for simultaneous offensives on January 5, 1942. The offensives were to take place in three areas: Moscow, Leningrad, and southern Russia. Zhukov, the highest-ranking Russian military leader, objected, but Stalin overruled those objections.

Stalin's offensives did not meet with success as the Red Army was chronically undersupplied, and the Germans were tactically superior. The Red Army lasted through multiple battles, including the Second Battle of Kharkov, and endured the crushing depletion of personnel and equipment in conflict near Rzhev. At Rzhev, both sides suffered continual losses, which earned the conflict the name the "Rzhev meat grinder." As both armies failed to achieve any decisive outcome, the stage was set for a massive change of momentum that would be brought about by the Battle of Stalingrad.

Leading up to the Battle of Stalingrad, while the Germans had not succeeded in taking Moscow or Leningrad, they were still a formidable threat, and no power was certain as to which side would prevail. The Russians had spared their capital, but the Germans continued to engage in offensives. As Germany anticipated the entrance of other nations into World War II, it also contemplated a shift in strategy. Instead of focusing on the conquest of Moscow and Leningrad, it instead looked toward shoring up its interests in natural resources in the southern parts of Russia. Germany understood that the precious natural resource—especially oil—would be crucial in maintaining its war efforts.

As the German army shifted its attention away from Moscow, it moved toward the Caucasus. Although there is debate as to whether the German army truly needed to capture and occupy the city itself, Hitler ordered that the city not be bypassed but rather that it be completely subdued. Some historians suggest that the reason the city was hotly contested was that it was named for the supreme Soviet leader himself and that both sides were more interested in the symbolism that pertained to the city rather than to any strategy that might be advanced by its capture. Hitler hated Stalin and all things Stalin, and Stalin did not want his namesake city to be captured by the Germans.

As Hitler threatened the city, every citizen who was able took up arms against the German invaders. German Army Groups A and B became distant from each other as Army Group B pursued the attack against Stalingrad. In fighting to the north of Stalingrad, Soviet soldiers made a desperate effort to slow the advance of the German army. Civilians were trapped in the city, as Stalin was unwilling to admit defeat and evacuate them. Even as German soldiers were attacking plants within the city, those plants were finishing armaments to be used against the Germans. The Germans bombarded the city, rendering the local Russian air assets unusable and the river impassable. The German advance through the outer perimeters of Stalingrad was painfully slow.

On September 5, 1942, the Russian forces attempted to attack the XIV Panzer Corps. The German air force proved to be an important asset in the fight, and the Russian forces were left with a mere 20,000 personnel dug into the center of the city. The bitter fight for every square inch of the city even included the sewers. It took the Germans over three months to nearly conquer the city. There were still strong pockets of resistance and the German army was faced with shortages due to increasing hostilities on other fronts. The Russian winter would also harass the tired Germans.

The Russian commanders turned their attention to the weaker German flanks, defended by soldiers with less experience and fewer resources. Although units along the German army's flanks asked to be repositioned, Hitler mandated that no ground be given up, not even for a strategic advantage. General Zhukov successfully organized his soldiers in Operation Uranus and attack the weaker German flanks. Then the Russians advanced as the Germans had not prepared any defensive positions behind their flanks. The weather inhibited German air operations. A second Soviet offensive attacked, heading toward Stalingrad from the opposite direction, and, on November 23, 1942, the Soviet forces met at the town of Kalach, encircling the entire German Sixth Army.

Fortunes had turned significantly by the same time a year later. Stalin had bolstered industrial production by moving industry beyond the reach of German forces. The Germans had lost much of their territorial gains. Stalin came to a meeting with Churchill and Roosevelt in November 1943 with the hope that the Allies would further tax the Germans by committing to a western front to aid the Soviet Union. The two western leaders clearly indicated that they would not open a western front, leaving Stalin angry. He had hoped that Allied help would provide a respite for his war-weary forces. 1944 would bring slow advances against the Germans as Russian forces learned from their mistakes and refined their tactics. The Russians also reaped the benefits of scarce resources on the German side. As Soviet soldiers conquered more German controlled territory, they began setting the stage for the post-World War II Cold War. As the Red Army marched through different areas, it left behind pre-communist governments that answered to Stalin.

SECTION 4.3: THE IMPACT OF THE WAR

The war in Europe ended on May 8, 1945, and all hostilities ended across the globe on September 2, 1945. The Russian people celebrate May 9 as Victory Day, a day which is sacred to the Russian people. Some have asserted that the war had touched every Russian family. The nation had given millions of its citizen in an effort to stave off the Nazis. The over fifty million military and civilian casualties were by themselves staggering. On top of the prodigious deaths of millions, the survivors were left with permanent physical and emotional scars that cannot be quantified. Thousands of villages literally disappeared along with broad swathes of the nation's agricultural and industrial production. Thousands of factories and thousands of miles of railways and communications lines had been destroyed. The utter destruction ushered in a time of famine after the end of the war, as there simply was not the manpower or the equipment to grow crops.

As the war came to an end, Stalin had matured as a leader. He had successfully appealed to his nation's patriotism to resist the blitzkrieg when other nations had been paralyzed by fear. Much like Winston Churchill's speeches had galvanized the beleaguered English during the Battle of Britain, Stalin had united the nation against a common enemy. Stalin had appealed to traditional Russian beliefs and had even liberalized his policies toward religion during the war. When the church supported Stalin against the Germans, Stalin allowed the church to choose its first patriarch, or leader, in thirty years. This permissive attitude toward the church meant that a widespread religious revival occurred as individuals appealed to a higher power than Stalin to save them from the Germans. Additionally, Stalin had come to respect the expertise of his military leaders, allowing them to direct the war's progress towards its final stages. Importantly, Stalin viewed the Soviet conquest of former German territory as a means by which to secure communist influence over the eastern part of Europe.

Stalin was clearly looking to the future of his nation as he rebuilt. Stalin leveraged the prisoners of war and the opponents of his regime as forced labor to jump start the Russian economy again. Stalin also seized German assets to help recover Russian industrial production, and he began setting the stage for Soviet power to increase in the coming decades.

SECTION 4.4: SETTLEMENTS OF WWII AND THE ORIGINS OF THE COLD WAR

Stalin had clashed with western nations over spheres of influence as early as 1943. Part of his disagreement at Tehran in 1943 was over the fate of Iran which was then partially controlled by Russia and partially by Britain. In 1945, when the Allied leaders met at the Yalta Conference in February, no consensus was reached as to how the German nation would be treated after the war. Stalin, Churchill, and Roosevelt met for a second time. Leaders faced disagreements over whether Germany would have to pay reparations and whether Poland would retain sovereignty. The agreement reached at Yalta was weak, although it marked the most significant level of cooperation between the three powers. The powers pledged to respect democracy in the liberated nations and to commit to building an acceptable Polish government. Stalin promised to enter the war against Japan when the Allied leaders agreed that he should get back territory that had been under Russian rule before the Russo-Japanese War.

After Victory in Europe Day on May 8, 1945, the Allied leaders again met at Potsdam in Germany to discuss the fate of the country. The American presidency had passed to Harry S. Truman, who had no history of dealing with Stalin. Truman relied on advisors who were not as friendly toward the Soviet leader as Roosevelt had been. Leadership of Britain had also changed, with the nation being represented by Clement Attlee.

After the Potsdam Conference had taken place, the United States successfully detonated atomic bombs on the cities of Hiroshima and Nagasaki, Japan. The Soviets felt threatened by this development as the United States was now in possession of superior military technology. The ensuing reconstruction of Japan under U.S. influence gave Stalin little motivation to pursue a better relationship with the United States with the ending the shipments of goods from the U.S. to Russia, even though the nation faced huge challenges in supplying the basic needs of its people.

Soviet Russia responded to the perceived threat by solidifying its grasp on what would become known as the Eastern Bloc. The nations that would make up the Eastern Bloc were commonly viewed as satellite states of the Soviet Union. Although they were not part of the Soviet Union in theory, they were clearly affiliated with and followed the lead of the Soviet Union.

In the years directly after World War II, the Soviets tried to maintain a veneer of democracy in the governance of these countries. However, all key positions were dominated by members of the communist party, and measures were implemented across the Eastern Bloc to destroy capitalist practices, including private ownership of land.

In 1947, the United States began in earnest to rebuild Europe through the Marshall Plan, The Marshall Plan proposed that assistance be given to all European countries rebuilding after the war. Eastern Bloc countries such as Czechoslovakia and Poland rejected the offers of aid after pressure from Moscow. From this point, the thin veneer of democracy crumbled.

Stalin ordered the nations under his sphere of influence to leave the Paris Conference in the European Recovery Program in July of 1947. Those opposing the communist rule of their nations faced open persecution from that moment forward.

 Section 5: Post-war Stalinism

SECTION 5.1: RECONSTRUCTION

Stalin set about rebuilding the Russian economy with a new five-year plan in 1945. This five-year plan was the fourth five-year plan. Under this plan, Stalin hoped to establish the Soviet Union as the leading industrial power of the world by 1960. Every single sector of the Russian economy was producing less than its pre-war levels. While Russia had hoped to gain aid from the United States immediately after the war, it soon became clear that the United States did not have any intention of sending large amounts of aid to the ravaged nation. Instead, the Soviet Union had to make do with reparations from Germany and economic payments from the Eastern Bloc countries. The Russian nation also benefited from forced labor in the form of German prisoners of war. Again, heavy industrialization received the emphasis while consumer goods were ignored.

The Marshall Plan, with the official title of the European Recovery Program (ERP), was the product of extensive advocacy on the part of George Marshall. The plan itself was largely a formulation of ideas from state department officials William L. Clayton and George F. Kennan. Marshall had held the highest rank possible in the United States Army: General of the Army, and had served as Chief of Staff of the United States Army during World War II. After the war, Marshall served as the United States Secretary of State for President Truman, beginning in the early part of 1947. Marshall began advocating for the ERP on June 5, 1947 during a speech at Harvard. The aims of the plan were to efficiently and expeditiously rebuild the European economy, exerting American influence on Western Europe. The Soviets reacted to the plan with a prohibition against Eastern Bloc country participation.

Marshall's address at Harvard described the difficulties that Europe faced. He urged the adoption of the plan as a means by which the American ideals of individual liberty and free government could exist. Marshall effectively communicated how he hoped that economic recovery would bring about stability in the European continent. While the speech was able to motivate European leaders to work together, the speech itself had few details of what the plan would entail. Indeed, the United States government tried to distract the American people from Marshall's speech, believing that the public would not support this type of involvement after such a costly war.

As the United States began rallying support amongst the European nations, the Soviets refused to allow the Eastern Bloc countries to attend as detailed above. In reaction to the coordination occurring in the American sphere of influence, the Soviet Union organized a campaign against the plan, labeling it as an attempt by the Americans to enslave Europeans. The communist parties actively opposed any non-communist ideal, even outside of the Marshall Plan. The communist parties in nations such as France and Italy were directly tasked by Stalin to try to undermine the plan and to oppose any domestic policy.

When the American legislature took up the Marshall Plan, the plan enjoyed support from both parties, and a first bill promising $5 billion in aid was passed. The American public, along with the American legislature, accepted the idea that ongoing poverty in Europe would only provide a breeding ground for communism. They also recognized that the plan would likely stimulate America's own growth.

Negotiation of the details of the plan was difficult to achieve. Each European nation had its own interests, and the Americans were wary of driving any other countries into the waiting arms of the Soviet Union. Truman explicitly recognized the Soviet Union's refusal to help the American-lead ERP and, while the Soviets sulked, American money began flowing into the treasuries of European nations. Much of the money was in turn spent on importing American goods.

The nations needed immediate aid in purchasing basic items such as food, raw materials, feed for livestock, and farming tools. However, as time passed, the money was also increasingly spent on the rebuilding of European militaries. The money was given to countries that had been on both sides of the war. Britain received the largest portion of the aid, while France and Germany were respectively the second and third largest recipients of aid. Although the plan officially ended in 1951, the United States continued to aid the Western European nations in other ways.

Scholars disagree over how much effect the Marshall Plan had, but Europe saw massive economic growth and recovery over the next twenty years, bringing the standard of living in Western Europe to record levels. The plan also exported American culture, including music and film, to the Western European nations, exerting its own cultural influence over the countries who received aid.

Although the plan did not completely live up to the hopes of George Marshall, it did make large strides toward integrating the countries of Europe and opened trade barriers that had previously existed between the nations.

Where the Western European nations were receiving aid and support from the United States, the Soviet Union, which had lost a quarter of its industry, clawed its way out of the destruction. To put their challenges in perspective, as mentioned before, the Soviet Union had lost millions of citizens. Even after hostilities ceased, famine swept the land as both the people and the equipment needed to grow crops had been destroyed. Even by 1959, the traces of the war could still be seen—in the population over the age of 35, there were nearly twice as many women as there were men. No other nation had lost as much.

Despite these massive challenges, Russia emerged as a superpower after the war. Although it was not accepting money from the Marshall Plan, Russia leveraged its control over Eastern Europe to boost its global position. From Germany, Russia removed both the equipment from German factories and the engineers that had designed the equipment. Using its central authority, the government, still led by Stalin, initiated new five-year plans that emphasized the growth of heavy industry and arms production. The satellite countries of Eastern Europe had to provide raw materials.

Stalin exerted an iron grip on the people after the war, justifying his actions by pointing toward the United States as a direct threat. While he had been liberal in his approach toward the Russian Orthodox Church during the war, Stalin reversed course. Churches and capitalists once again faced persecution. Citizens who had lived outside of the Soviet Union during the war were viewed with extreme distrust, even if they had been taken out of the country as prisoners of war. These individuals faced Stalin's Gulag or even execution upon their return. Even those who had entered the communist party during the war faced purges.

SECTION 5.2: NATIONALISM

For the nations of Western Europe, nationalism was an idea to be avoided after the concept was used by Hitler to justify his actions. As the nations wanted to distance themselves from the negative side of nationalism, they were more receptive to organizations that would pursue the collective benefit for a group.

One of the consequences of this change in mindset was the movement away from colonialism at the end of World War II. Before the war, European nations exerted control over distant parts of the world through colonial rule. Britain released its colonies soon after World War II. France would also eventually follow Britain's example. As the colonies began their own self-government, there was instability as the world watched to see which countries would exert the most influence over these newly minted governments. As the United States would learn, as it experienced conflicts in Asia, the destabilization of these trends would last for years.

Even as many colonial powers let go of their colonies, Russia pursued an opposite course. Russia shamelessly exported its nationalism to its satellite nations. Before World War II, key leaders like Lenin had rejected nationalist tendencies in favor of ideological allegiances. However, the brutality of the war motivated Stalin to favor Russian nationalism as a unifying force. Not only were the people fighting for survival as communists, they were also fighting for the survival of Russia. Stalin would leverage this newfound Russian nationalism for the rest of his tenure.

SECTION 5.3: ARMS RACE

The United States exited World War II with military technology that other nations, especially Russia, envied. Stalin had known of the United States' development of the atomic bomb even before the weapon had been completed. This sensitive topic was raised as early as 1946, when the United Nations met for the first time. The United Nations, an intergovernmental organization, was founded in order to prevent another conflict like World War II. The United States was eager to preserve its dominant position in having the new technology and proposed that atomic weapons be monitored. Soviets pushed for abolition of nuclear weapons. Neither position was adopted by the United Nations. The United States had hoped that they would maintain a nuclear advantage over the Russians and keep their European ambitions in check.

The United States would continue to test nuclear weapons while the Russians worked feverishly to develop their own nuclear weapons. American experts did not expect the Soviets to complete nuclear weapons until the mid-1950s; however, the Soviets worked hard and enjoyed the help of spies working in the United States' program. The Russians detonated their first nuclear weapon on August 29, 1949.

Both superpowers increased spending to improve their nuclear weapons, and an arms race ensued, with both sides trying to outpace the other in the development of nuclear weapons. Both nations also spent large amounts of money developing technologies that could deliver nuclear weapons or defend against the delivery of such weapons. Both nations amassed arsenals of long range bombers, missiles, and submarines designed with the purpose of delivering the nuclear threat. There also had to be defensive weapons systems like fighter jets to defend against the threats. Eventually, this obsession with nuclear delivery resulted in the space race and the Soviet launch of Sputnik.

SECTION 5.4: COLD WAR IN EUROPE

The term "Cold War" was possibly coined by the famous author George Orwell who authored classics like *Animal Farm* and *1984*. The term referred to nations that were clearly aligned against other nations but were not pursuing open and active hostilities against enemies. The phrase was then used by Bernard Baruch, a presidential advisor. Whatever the origin of the term, it aptly described the relationship between the United States and Russia after World War II. Neither power would directly confront the other, but instead the two engaged in an arms race, proxy wars, and the strengthening of their own spheres of influence.

As the Allies gained space from the Axis threat, there was less need for unity, and different visions of a post-World War II nation began to emerge. Some of the Allies shared democratic governments that guaranteed individual freedoms as contrasted with the Soviet Union. The United States was aware of its rising status in the global economy and sought to cement that status. The United States also desired to create the international body that would become the United Nations so as to prevent future conflict. Winston Churchill was interested in the British Empire, and he was very concerned about the stability of Europe especially creating a buffer between Western European nations and Russia. In essence, Britain and the United States did not at first share a common strategy toward Russia, and Churchill made separate agreements with Stalin that did not involve the United States.

When President Roosevelt died in April 1945, Harry S. Truman became the next president. Truman had not been involved in Roosevelt's dealings with Stalin, and Truman brought much more suspicion into his relationship with the Soviet leader. He was especially wary of Stalin when it became clear that Stalin intended to plant a Soviet government in Poland, despite the fact that there was a Polish government operating in exile. As the Nazis retreated, the Soviets had fallen into their pre-war territory, which had been assigned under the Molotov-Ribbentrop Pact.

The line between the United States and Russia became clear when Russia seemed to accuse the United States of preparing to conquer the world for its capitalist interests. The United States fired back, asserting that it was going to keep its military in Europe for the foreseeable future. Famously, Winston Churchill delivered a speech in March 1946 referencing the lines that had been drawn across the continent of Europe. After this moment, the term "iron curtain" referred to the border separating the Western European nations from the Soviet sphere of influence.

In 1947, Truman announced a doctrine of containment to counter the growth of communism when it became clear that the communists were seeking to exert more influence in countries like Greece and were not at all receptive to the American ideas on nuclear development. Truman appealed to his countrymen's ideals by painting the developing Cold War as a conflict between freedom and a tyrannical dictatorship. This concept would become known as the Truman Doctrine, and the strategies of containing and deterring the communist threat were embraced by both political parties in the United States. If the Truman Doctrine was the stick, then the Marshall Plan was the carrot.
Stalin reacted to these policies by creating Cominform, a body to ensure that the communist parties in the Eastern Bloc countries adhered to the party dogma. Stalin also brutally crushed a coup in Czechoslovakia. Despite Stalin's efforts, not all satellite nations followed in a docile manner. The Socialist Federal Republic of Yugoslavia, under the leadership of Josip Broz Tito, successfully escaped the Russian sphere of influence. Tito had rejected a resolution of Cominform in 1948 and refused to take more direction from Moscow.

Tito advocated for his own brand of communism that would be named Titoism in his honor. Tito's version of communism promoted the idea that individual countries must look at their own situations to determine how communist ideals could be best reached in their own countries. Tito rejected the centralized direction of Stalin and pursued his own communist ideals in ways that clashed with Moscow's direction.

Soviet leaders branded Tito as a heretic and follower of Trotsky, but Tito was a strong leader. Much of the tension in the relationship came from Tito's view of himself as an ally with, and not a subordinate to, Stalin. Tito was also able to see his country as more independent because Yugoslavia had received little help from the Red Army when it had liberated itself from Axis armies. When Russian later formulated the Warsaw Pact, Yugoslavia would not join. While Yugoslavia viewed itself as staunchly socialist, it maintained its independence through the collapse of the Soviet Union. Despite how Tito viewed himself, the Soviet Union labeled him as a western ally in its propaganda machine. Tito did borrow from the Soviet Union in that he also persecuted those who opposed his regime, sending opponents to his own prison camp at Goli Otok.

The differences between the Soviet Union and the United States eventually lead to formal declarations. In 1949, NATO, or the North Atlantic Treaty Organization, was formed. This treaty was a military agreement between North American powers and Western Europe, with the purpose of providing collective defense against the Soviet threat. The Berlin Blockade of 1948 had motivated the nations to consider their security when the Soviets had refused to allow food and other crucial aid into the non-Russian parts of Berlin.

From the beginning, the organization's mission focused on containing the Russian threat, and under the agreement the nations who entered into the treaty, would view any attack on one as an attack on all of the nations. The Western European nations considered this essential against the Russian control of the Eastern Bloc. The goals of the treaty were also the product of Atlanticism, which emphasized mutual cooperation and close ties between the nations in North America and the Western Europeans.

NATO may not have gained traction as an organization if it had not been for the start of the Korean War in 1950. Prior to the war, the Soviet Union occupied the northern part of Korea, and the United States occupied the southern part of the peninsula. Both northern and southern Korea had separate governments that each claimed to be the legitimate government of the nation. North Korean forces, bolstered by communist support from both the Russian and Chinese government, attacked the South on June 25, 1950. The Russians had boycotted the United Nations Security Council meeting that resolved to send aid to Korea. If they had been present, the resolution may not have failed, and the nations could have avoided the conflict. The Korean War, often termed the Forgotten War, saw the use of napalm on civilian populations. Prior to his removal as commander, General Douglas MacArthur had even suggested the use of the nuclear bomb. However, cooler heads prevailed; the nuclear weapon was never used.

The rest of the world realized the potential danger of unified communist action, spurring a strengthening of NATO. Leaders began using NATO as the means to develop specific military plans to anticipate a communist threat. The military preparation culminated in military exercises. By the end of 1952, the navies of NATO members participated in a joint exercise to simulate the response to a possible threat on Denmark and Norway. The naval exercise was soon followed by exercises for ground forces, and included the simulation of potential nuclear warfare. Eventually, Greece and Turkey joined the organization in 1952, bringing the total membership to fourteen countries: Belgium, the Netherlands, France, the United Kingdom, Luxembourg, Portugal, Italy, the United States, Canada, Norway, Denmark, Iceland, Greece, and Italy.

The Soviet Union watched as the NATO countries made strides to unify their military equipment, technology, and planning. In determining how best to handle the growing unification on the western side of the Iron Curtain, the Soviet Union proposed in 1954 that it join NATO. The leaders of NATO rejected the proposal and seemingly escalated the tension between Moscow and the west by releasing the MC 48. MC 48 was a document promulgated by NATO's military committee that spelled out NATO's potential reactions to Soviet aggression. Under the guidance of the document, the NATO forces openly addressed war with the Soviet Union and clearly indicated that it anticipated using nuclear weapons from the outset of the conflict to prevent communist forces from overrunning Europe. With its wartime doctrine established, NATO then allowed West Germany to enter its organization on May 9, 1955. The implications of rearming West Germany were not lost on the Soviet Union.

In response to the growing tension with NATO, the Soviet Union formed the Warsaw Pact almost immediately. On May 14, 1955, leaders of the Soviet Union and communist bloc countries signed a mutual defense agreement similar in purpose to NATO. The agreement's official title was The Treaty of Friendship, Co-operation and Mutual Assistance. Signed in Poland, the treaty originally included the following nations: Albania, Bulgaria, Czechoslovakia, East Germany, Hungary, Poland, Romania, and the Soviet Union. The nations were sovereign in theory, and the agreement acknowledged that they should not interfere in the internal affairs of the other member nations. However, it soon became clear that the Soviet Union would leverage the agreement to exert even more control over the Eastern Bloc countries. The Soviet Union justified further meddling into the military affairs of the member nations with the Warsaw Pact. The Soviet interest in the militaries of the Warsaw Pact nations would be the excuse that allowed the Russian army to suppress uprising in Hungary and Czechoslovakia when those countries challenged Soviet authority. After the end of communist power in Russia in Eastern Europe, governments were able to withdraw from the pact, and it officially ended in 1991.

SECTION 5.5: COLD WAR IN ASIA

While NATO and the Warsaw Pact countries did not engage in direct hostilities toward one another for decades, proxy wars carried the conflict between the signatories to different parts of the world. A proxy war takes place when a conflict is encouraged by a nation that never takes part in the war itself. Basically, these proxy wars centered on the Soviet Union stirring up conflict in other nations in the hopes of working contrary to NATO interests and involving other powers. Much of this desire to engage in proxy warfare was inspired by the major powers' fears of total nuclear war if they were to challenge each other directly. Additionally, toward the end of the Cold War, superpowers wanted to avoid the expense of using their expensive armaments, and they found it cheaper to arm the combatants in the smaller, poorer countries with less costly weapons. Another aspect of the proxy war was the toll that long, open conflict had on the popular opinion of superpowers. Both Russia and the United States experienced sociopolitical retaliation as their people grew tired of ongoing conflict in Afghanistan and Vietnam respectively.

Pro-American countries such as the Philippines and Thailand reaped the benefit of American support; however, the Soviet Union tried to maintain a large sphere of influence across Asia. U.S. military forces still maintained installations in nations like Japan and the Philippines after the end of World War II, giving the United States secure launching points for operations.

The key proxy wars in Asia were Korea and Vietnam, but the Soviet Union influenced many of the countries in the region. Indeed, the nations of Kazakhstan, Afghanistan, and Uzbekistan were merely states in the Soviet Union, having no sovereignty of their own. Many other smaller conflicts in Asia received arms and advisors from both sides of the Cold War as the Soviet Union tried to gain power in the vacuum left by the end of European colonialism.

While China lurked in the background of the Asian conflicts, it had to solve its own internal problems at the start of the Cold War. Mao Zedong was struggling to consolidate his own power and did not see himself as a subordinate to Stalin. Mao was also conducting his infamous cultural revolution from the mid-sixties until the mid-seventies which strained the Chinese society. During the Cold War, Chinese interests never completely aligned with the Soviet Union.

Section 6: The Khrushchev Years

SECTION 6.1: SUCCESSION STRUGGLE

The end of World War II marked the high point for Stalin's reputation as a leader at home and internationally. However, as the war came to an end and Stalin's health began to fail, he continued his habits of repressing any group or person that he deemed as a threat. This included groups of people in the newly conquered Eastern Bloc and loyal followers like Molotov. In the turnover at the departure of Molotov, Nikita Khrushchev became an important figure. Khrushchev took over the important post of Central Committee Secretary of the Moscow Communist Party.

In 1953, Stalin died. He had not groomed any one person to succeed him, and the nation was left to watch as party leaders competed for the role. In the vacuum left by Stalin's death, Khrushchev would have to overtake four different competitors: Beria, Kaganovich, Bulganin, and Molotov. Immediately after Stalin's death, Georgy Malenkov had been named as the Chairman of the Council of Ministers alongside Beria, Kaganovich, Bulganin, and Molotov. As leaders were very suspicious of Malenkov having too much power, Malenkov resigned on March 14, 1953. His resignation left room for Khrushchev's ascent into power. Perhaps because Khrushchev was viewed as an ignorant outsider, the established power structure did not see him as a threat.

Beria was soon eliminated as a threat to Khrushchev. Beria, who exercised absolute control over all security agencies at the time, began a campaign of reform to counter Stalin's personality cult. He advocated for the freeing of labor camp internees and other reforms. As Beria planned ambitious changes, Khrushchev united with Malenkov against the head of the secret police. Much of this was motivated by the fear that Beria was going to organize a military coup. Leadership organized the arrest of Beria in June of 1953, and, by the end of the year, Beria and his closest supporters were executed. On a brighter note, Beria was the last Soviet leader executed in the power struggle over the highest offices of the nation.

With Beria gone, Malenkov tried to reassert the power of the communist party which had waned under Stalin. Stalin had assumed much of the power himself, and Khrushchev viewed the party's return to power as detrimental to his own interests. Khrushchev began grooming party officials who would support him. He also used his personal charm to win supporters. While his manners were unsophisticated, he carried himself with a very practical, approachable manner. Khrushchev also leveraged his possession of secret files taken from Beria. These files would show his political opponent's involvement in Stalin's misdeeds.

Malenkov's lesser status became apparent when Khrushchev began taking the most important seat at the table for important meetings, and Khrushchev cemented his grasp on power when he was able to place his own nominee in charge of the KGB.

Khrushchev's maneuvering culminated with the Central Committee's formal resolution accusing Malenkov of being party to Stalin's crimes against the Russian people. Malenkov lost all real power, and Khrushchev was firmly ensconced as head of the USSR. Nikolai Bulganin took Malenkov's position as Chairman of the Council of Ministers.

SECTION 6.2: DE-STALINIZATION

While Khrushchev was solidifying his place of power, the country was quietly trying to deal with the aftermath of Stalin's brutal regime. From 1953 until 1955, this was a very quiet movement. In later periods, the criticism of Stalin would be much more open. This trend toward both passively or openly rejecting Stalin and his actions became known as de-Stalinization. There were several different manifestations of this movement. This movement began cautiously, as many communists held Stalin in high repute, both inside and outside of the Soviet Union. Changes were made in the government with no explanation being offered. Stalin's policies were reversed. Persons who had been condemned and maligned under Stalin's regime began to receive favorable treatment. Prisoners returned from labor camps.

As time passed, leaders became more open in their challenges to Stalin's legacy. Khrushchev moved to begin an investigation into Stalin's practices. The results were shocking. According to the investigation, almost two million people were arrested for anti-Soviet actions. These charges against these individuals were illegitimate and generally fictional. Of the nearly two million arrested for these types of offenses against the Soviet state, nearly 700,000 were executed after confessing to crimes because of torture.

Khrushchev brought the issues into relief with his speech entitled "On the Cult of Personality and its Consequences." Khrushchev gave this speech to a session of the 20th Party Congress of the Communist Party of the Soviet Union on February 25, 1956. This speech was unexpected and highly controversial. In the speech, Khrushchev decried Stalin's cult of personality as being opposed to the ideals of the Soviet Union. Khrushchev further had the audacity to accuse Stalin of being a dictator. Khrushchev even alleged that Stalin's execution of Bolshevik leaders who had taken part in the October Revolution was criminal and that Stalin's accomplices, especially Beria, were responsible with Stalin for perpetrating crimes.

While scholars differ as to why Khrushchev was motivated to give the speech, it signaled dramatic changes across Russian society. Some believe that Khrushchev truly wanted a return to communist ideals. Others, however, believe that Khrushchev merely wanted to avoid blame for Stalin's reign of terror. The most dramatic effect of the movement was to reform the Gulag system. Under Khrushchev's leadership, the Gulag shrank to a much smaller size. Small freedoms that had been prohibited before, such as correspondence with family or receipt of clothing from the outside, were permitted. Eventually, the Gulag was closed on January 25, 1960. The Troikas that had summarily inflicted punishment on those who were charged with anti-Soviet crimes were disbanded. Another change effected by the speech was the eradication of Stalin's name from many features of the culture. Stalin's name vanished from buildings, institutions, landmarks, and even songs. Monuments to the dictator disappeared overnight in some places, or were replaced. Stalin's body was removed from public display where it had enjoyed a prominent position near Lenin's body.

De-Stalinization remained a sensitive subject, and, while Khrushchev was able to make significant changes in how the nation viewed the former leader, opinions would vary as the USSR's policy moved between extremes. Khrushchev's action would become known as the Khrushchev Thaw, a time in which the intensity of the Cold War diminished for a moment. The Soviet people were able to enjoy more access to consumer goods and enjoyed slightly more freedom of speech and the freedom of the press. Unfortunately, when Khrushchev passed from power in 1964, these changes seemed to end, and the Cold War became cold again.

SECTION 6.3: SOVIET RELATIONS WITH THE U.S. UNDER KHRUSHCHEV

Under Khrushchev, the USSR experienced dramatic extremes in its relationship with the U.S. Khrushchev permitted a liberalization of policies that allowed his citizens to travel. He was interested in working toward a solution for the conflicts that divided Europe into two spheres of influence. Khrushchev was very concerned about the West Berlin presence in the Russian-influenced East Germany. He tried to pressure the western powers into giving up the enclave. While he would set deadlines for the western nations to come to an agreement with East Germany, he would also extend the deadlines when it became obvious that they were not going to be met.

Khrushchev postured militarily to the western powers. He believed that he needed to improve his nation's nuclear arsenal, but at the same time he doubted whether the USSR needed large conventional forces to defend itself from the western threat. Khrushchev's desire to enhance the USSR's missile program led to his nation's aggressive space program. To the surprise and shock of the United States, his country was able to beat the Americans in the launch of Sputnik. Sputnik was the first manmade satellite to orbit the earth. These advances spurred other nations to follow suit. Khrushchev had shrewdly preceded many visits to foreign countries with missile tests, and the true state of the

Soviet missile program was not really known until the United States was able to fly spy planes over the country.

In 1959, Vice President Richard Nixon visited the Soviet Union. During this visit, Nixon and Khrushchev would engage in a debate over the merits of their respective government systems, inspired by a visit to an exhibition that purported to show the model American kitchen at the American National Exhibition in Russia. This exchange led to Khrushchev's visit to the United States in September 1959. Khrushchev was able to sample many facets of American culture during his visit, including visits to major cities and President Eisenhower's farm. The U.S. president was able to reach an informal agreement with the USSR's leader during these interactions. The two decided not to impose a definite deadline for the Berlin situation. Instead, they intended to hold a four-party summit to discuss the issue. Khrushchev left the United States believing that he had achieved a personal relationship with President Eisenhower and that he could reach an agreement to his liking on the Berlin issue.

Events unfolding high above the USSR would deter the four-party talks. The U.S. had regularly flown U-2 spy planes over the USSR's territory. On April 9, 1960, the U.S. resumed the flights after a pause. Khrushchev did not want to think that Eisenhower would engage in these tactics after establishing a personal relationship. Khrushchev assumed that Eisenhower was not aware of the operations. Finally, on May 1, 1960, the USSR was able to shoot one of the spy planes down.

The United States reacted to the plane's loss by saying that a weather plane had crashed. The United States did not think that the pilot had survived. Khrushchev announced on May 5 that the airplane that had been lost was actually a U.S. spy plane and that the Soviet Union had the pilot in custody. Khrushchev, holding onto his belief that Eisenhower had not approved the flyover, condemned the U.S. military power structure. Eisenhower, however, admitted that he had endorsed the mission. These events were unfolding mere days before Khrushchev was set to engage in the four-party talks. At the summit, Khrushchev took the position that the U.S. should apologize and desist from flying any more missions over Soviet territory. Eisenhower's response was less than satisfying to Khrushchev. Eisenhower responded that flights had been suspended, and the president invited Khrushchev to endorse a policy of mutual flyovers. Khrushchev insisted that there was no purpose in continuing the Paris Summit and posited that the summit should be rescheduled for a future date that would fall after the next American election. Eisenhower opined that Khrushchev had sabotaged the summit, and Khrushchev revoked his invitation for Eisenhower to visit the Soviet Union.

Khrushchev's image was also severely tarnished by his second and final trip to the United States. In September 1960, Khrushchev came to the United States as the leader of the USSR's delegation to the United Nations. Khrushchev was interested in extending Soviet influence to the newly independent nations of the Third World. The

Soviet Union proposed a resolution to condemn colonialization. A Philippine delegate responded to the resolution by asking the Soviet Union why it was condemning colonialism while the Soviet Union was engaging in virtually the same conduct in regard to its influence over Eastern Europe. Khrushchev interrupted the delegate and demanded to respond, saying that the Philippines were merely under the control of the American capitalists. The delegate continued his speech, drawing attention to the Soviet Union's hypocrisy. While the delegate was still talking, Khrushchev proceeded to take his shoe off and bang it on the table in anger. Khrushchev's rudeness embarrassed many of his own countrymen.

John F. Kennedy was elected to be the president of the United States in 1960. Khrushchev viewed this as favorable at first because he had believed that Vice President Nixon would have taken a much more aggressive stance against the Soviet Union. However, Kennedy proved to be less friendly than Khrushchev had hoped. Khrushchev took comfort in the fact that his nation was shortly thereafter able to launch the first humans into space. Kennedy also faced humiliation when a CIA-sponsored group of Cuban exiles tried to attack Cuba in the Bay of Pigs debacle.

On April 17, 1961, a group of Cuban exiles who opposed Cuba's communist leader, Fidel Castro, attempted to invade Cuba with the help of the CIA. As the 1950s had come to a close, Castro had grown close to the Soviet Union, and the close proximity of the island to the United States had made President Eisenhower nervous. With American air support, over 1,400 personnel attempted to invade. Castro himself eventually began directing operations against the invasion, and Kennedy grew timid as the operation attracted negative attention. Kennedy was willing to provide less support than the CIA had estimated would be necessary. Without crucial air and sea assets, the invasion ended within three days.

Kennedy entered the Vienna Summit on June 3, 1961, with tensions between the nations at an all-time high. Neither side was willing to concede to the other. Khrushchev took a new approach and ordered Walter Ulbricht to build the Berlin Wall. The Berlin Wall would encompass the entirety of West Berlin. Early on a Sunday morning, the construction began, and with it ended any hope that the four nations could come to a consensus concerning the state of affairs in Germany.

The next crisis in the relationship between the Soviets and the Americans came in 1962 when Russia planted medium-range missiles in Cuba only ninety miles from the American shore. When they were discovered by U-2 spy planes, Kennedy decided he would inform his nation about the looming crisis. While the Americans feared missile launches, Russia feared that American would invade their ally. Khrushchev would eventually agree to an American bargain to remove the missiles. While America would agree to remove its own missiles in Turkey, within striking distance of the Russia nation, that part of the deal was not announced to the public. Khrushchev appeared to be a weaker leader from that time forward.

SECTION 6.4: RIFT WITH CHINA

While relations with the United States experienced dramatic swings during Khrushchev's regime, Khrushchev ensured that the Soviet Union was exerting control over other areas of the world. Khrushchev would oversee the negotiations in Poland over Polish leadership. While Khrushchev dealt liberally with Poland, the USSR was far harsher in its treatment of Hungary when that nation attempted to leave the Warsaw Pact. In October 1956, the Hungarian people rebelled against the Soviet Union. The Soviet occupation responded with force, and both sides lost hundreds of lives. At first Khrushchev seemed to be taking a lax approach to Hungary. He withdrew his forces when a new premier, Imre Nagy, asked the Soviets to leave. Nagy soon faced Khrushchev's wrath after Nagy announced that democratic elections would take place and that Hungary would leave the Warsaw Pact. Russia invaded Hungary, killed thousands, and executed the rebellious leader. Khrushchev's notorious quote from the time was, "We will bury you."

In Asia, Mao Zedong had defeated all opponents in China and was seeking help from his fellow communists in Russia by 1949. By the end of the 1950s, Russia was pouring massive amounts of aid into the war-torn nation. Khrushchev even reached agreements with the Chinese relating to a return of territory that Russia had taken from China in the previous wars. When Mao was considering invading the island of Formosa, where his opposition would form its own government, Stalin discouraged the Chinese from attacking. Unfortunately, Mao began to disagree with the Soviet Union. Mao did not approve of the liberal approach that Khrushchev applied to Tito and Yugoslavia. Khrushchev had not challenged Tito's authority in Yugoslavia, and Mao did not view Tito's version of communism as pure. Additionally, Mao was angered by Khrushchev's secret speech. Perhaps the speech condemning the cult of personality struck a bit too close to home for the Chinese leader. In any case, Mao did not approve of the growing de-Stalinization in the USSR.

Mao actively sabotaged Russian-American relations by drawing the Americans into conflict over Taiwanese territory, and, as the Soviets noticed their interests diverging from those of the Chinese, the Soviets became less interested in sharing technology. By 1959, the Soviets decided against sharing their nuclear weapons plan with the Chinese. By 1960, the two countries were trading insults, and Khrushchev decided he should discontinue all aid to the Chinese. China and Russia had been driven apart by their own national interests and their differing views on how Marxist ideology should be applied. The Chinese accused the Russians of having counterrevolutionary trends when the Soviets acknowledged that they might want to peacefully coexist with the capitalist nations. Only after Henry Kissinger, the American Secretary of State, made a secret visit to China in 1971, was America able to begin opening relations with the Chinese.

SECTION 6.5: CHANGE OF POWER

Khrushchev was nearing the end of his reign in 1964. Leonid Brezhnev led the movement against Khrushchev. While Khrushchev spent considerable time away from the capital in 1964, Brezhnev was consolidating his support. Brezhnev found supporters in the First Deputy Premier, Alexander Shelepin, and the KGB Chairman, Vladimir Semichastny. Khrushchev realized that his power was at an end while surrounded by KGB security agents. He did not attempt to counter Brezhnev's power grab. Brezhnev's quiet coup was successful, and Khrushchev entered forced retirement.

With the switch in leaders, the USSR faced a return to more conservative policies from its leaders immediately after Khrushchev's removal. Brezhnev controlled the nation for nearly the next twenty years as the First Secretary of the Communist Party. Stalin was the only leader to be in power longer than Brezhnev.

Brezhnev successfully kept power by appearing to share power and by working to find agreement with members of the Politburo. Brezhnev, unlike Khrushchev, avoided quick decisions and was careful to gather opinions from other leaders before acting. Negatively, his long tenure resulted in corruption and an overall lack of economic development. His era is often referred to as the Brezhnev stagnation.

In theory, Brezhnev shared power with Nikolai Podgorny and Alexei Kosygin. However, it was clear that Brezhnev dominated the group. Alexander Shelepin did not approve of Brezhnev's strategy and tried to assume control himself in 1965, but Brezhnev easily survived the challenge, and Shelepin left his position in 1967. Brezhnev also increased his power as Mikhail Suslov and Alexei Kosygin decreased in influence.

Soon after Brezhnev's ascent to power, conservative policies began replacing the more liberal ones that had been allowed under his predecessor. These policies included repression of free thinkers, many of whom sought asylum in the west. Although Brezhnev's rule was not associated with the mass execution that Stalin had employed, Brezhnev allowed opponents to be jailed, ostensibly for mental illness. These "mentally ill" were generally those who opposed the regime or attempted to practice religion, a freedom not enjoyed by the Soviet people. With the support of Yuri Andropov, the head of the KGB, citizens feared arrest for expressing their opposition to the regime.

Defections from the Soviet Union called attention to the nation's habitual repression of its people's freedom, and contradicted Soviet propaganda that claimed to allow freedom in the nation. In June 1961, Rudolf Nureyev, a ballet prodigy, defected. As the Kirov Opera Ballet Company left Paris after a performance, Nureyev threw himself into the arms of a French airport security agent, begging not to return to Russia. Later, in 1974, Mikhail Baryshnikov, another famous ballet dancer, defected to Canada. These defections were embarrassing to the Soviet government.

The Soviet government also faced criticism from dissidents who vocally opposed the Soviet government's repression of free speech and other liberties enjoyed in the western nations. Among the dissidents, the author Aleksandr Solzhenitsyn is the most famous. Solzhenitsyn's book, *A Day in the Life of Ivan Denisovich*, described life in the Gulag. This work stood apart from all other literature produced in the Soviet Union because it was not written by a communist party member in a style that would glorify the government. He received the Nobel Prize for Literature in 1970, but he did not travel to Sweden to receive it because he feared that the Russian government would prevent his return. By 1974, the government forced Solzhenitsyn to leave the country. He would not be able to return until after the Soviet Union dissolved. Perhaps Solzhenitsyn's most important work was *The Gulag Archipelago*, which exposed the depths of Gulag suffering inflicted by Russians on their fellow countrymen.

Boris Pasternak's epic novel was another work that faced censorship by the regime: *Dr. Zhivago*. The novel appeared in 1957 and traced the life of the main character, Dr. Zhivago, as he navigates the First World War, the Russian Revolution, and the Russian Civil War while torn between his love for two different women. The Soviet leadership rejected the novel as it did not glorify the ideals of the revolution. The book was a prodigious international success and earned the Nobel Prize in 1958.

Yevgeny Yevtushenko was another famous dissident. By 1957, Yevtushenko was expelled from the official Russian literary circles because of his criticism for the regime. Yevtushenko's most famous poem, *Babi Yar*, exposed the persecution of the Jewish people by the Nazis as well as the Stalinist regime. Criticism of Stalin was a constant theme in Yevtushenko's works.

Roy and Zhores Medvedev were, respectively, a historian and a biologist who shared interests in opposing the Soviet regime. Zhores was interned in a mental asylum when the government determined that his views were contrary to their interests. Zhores also exposed the Soviet government's Kyshtym nuclear disaster. To this day, the disaster is the third-most serious nuclear accident in world history. The government was very secretive about the disaster and many people suffered the consequences as evacuations were slow. The government also tried to hide the disaster by creating a nature reserve which restricted access to the area. At first, many were skeptical of Zhores' report, but eventually his story was confirmed. Zhores' twin brother Roy published the anti-Stalinist work *Let History Judge*. Roy also published a work that revealed his brother's institutionalization, exposing the regime's persecution of dissidents. Along with the Medvedev brothers, Andrei Sakharov was a well-known dissident. A renowned nuclear physicist, Sakharov advocated for human rights, and these efforts led to his receipt of the Nobel Peace Prize in 1975.

SECTION 6.6: PROXY WARS

While Brezhnev was not openly pursuing conflict with western powers, he emphasized Russian military might. He diverted a large portion of his nation's GDP to military spending. There was an increasing arms race taking place between the Soviet Union and the western nations by the end of the 1970s, and this increased the tensions between the east and the west. Instead of using these weapons directly against the United States, Russia became involved in a series of proxy wars that indirectly involved the Soviet Union as the USSR funneled arms and advisors to nations opposing the American sphere of influence.

Brezhnev undertook diplomatic efforts with countries that were emerging in the post-colonial era. The USSR was eager to provide aid to the emerging nations. The countries did not identify the Soviet Union with their former colonial masters, and, in many cases, the countries were very willing to receive Soviet goods and ideas. Actions like the invasion of Egypt during the Suez Crisis often led countries to trust the Soviets over the former colonial superpowers. France and Britain had invaded the country to secure western control of the canal. American and Soviet leaders urged France and Britain to withdraw. However, Egypt was the one case where this rule did not stand true because Egyptian leader Anwar Sadat took an approach of openness toward the west in the 1970s.

During the era of the proxy wars and of the Cold War, the Soviet Union preferred to foment indirect conflicts as they were cheaper and had less risk of the use of nuclear weapons. Important proxy wars would emerge on every continent where the United States would either openly or secretly support one faction against another faction supported by the USSR. Famous examples would be the Korean War and the Vietnam War. Another example was the overthrowing of Chilean president, Salvador Allende. Allende came to power in 1970 after a contentious presidential race where no candidate gained a decisive number of votes. As Allende began implementing Marxist policies, including nationalization and collectivization, the United States' Central Intelligence Agency supported an effort to overthrow the Chilean president. The attempt to end Allende's communist policies backfired when the leader of the coup, General Pinochet, took power and became an abusive dictator in the country. The USSR intended these wars to diminish American popular support for the American war efforts.

SECTION 6.7: WAR IN AFGHANISTAN

Termed "Russia's Vietnam," the Russian invasion of Afghanistan proved to be a dreadful miscalculation on the part of the communists, and would be the most damaging proxy war to the Soviet reputation. The war in Afghanistan would linger for nearly a decade, costing the Soviets money, manpower, and materiel.

In 1978, a pro-Soviet government seized power in the country and formed an alliance with the USSR. The United States began sending aid to the opponents of this newly formed government.

This conflict was occurring against the backdrop of increased U.S. involvement in the Middle East. Egypt and Israel were making strides in their relationship, and the United States was also arming the Saudis. The Russians were concerned that the Americans were widening their sphere of influence very close to the Russian homeland.

The Soviet Union was happy to have the pro-communist leadership installed in Kabul. The Soviets did not recognize how the new government would stir up opposition. As the government attempted to make socialist reforms, many conservatives viewed the reforms as anti-Muslim. The new regulations concerning land and marriage directly contradicted religious traditions. As uprisings sprang up, the government stifled them violently. As foreign powers encouraged the Afghans to resolve their internal problems through negotiations, an American diplomat died in the crossfire between the two factions. The sides reached no peaceful resolution, and half of the Afghan army had defected to the rebellion by the end of 1980.

The pro-Soviet Afghan government called on the Russians to send forces under the terms of a treaty that they had signed with the Soviets in 1978. The government wanted aircraft and personnel, and the Soviets also sent tanks and ground forces to guard the airports from which the aircraft would operate. While some inside the Soviet Union opposed Russian intervention from the start, it soon became clear that the Soviet forces were being drawn into a larger involvement. The Afghans soon asked for entire units, not just crews.

Soviet leadership questioned the motives of Prime Minister Hafizullah Amin, suspecting that he was single-mindedly loyal to the Soviet Union. Amin furthered that suspicion when he began purging associates, including some who were loyal to the Soviet Union. The USSR made the decision to coordinate a large-scale invasion of the nation and replace the leaders with one that strictly answered to the Soviet Union. Using insiders to influence Afghan forces to take their equipment offline for maintenance and disrupting vital communication systems, the Russian forces assaulted Kabul on December 25, 1979. Soviet forces soon took strategic government buildings, including the Tajbeg Presidential Palace. In the assault, Amin died. The Russians immediately installed a puppet government, and introduced over 100,000 military personnel into the country. Jimmy Carter, the American president, demanded that the Americans boycott the 1980 Summer Olympics, held in Russia, as a response to the invasion.

For the first half of the 1980s the Soviets struggled, trapped in a pattern. The Soviets occupied major cities, but rural areas were under control of the Mujahedeen. This war faced condemnation from the entire world, but especially from Muslim countries. The Soviets did not help their side with their campaign of brute force that had no regard for civilians. Foreign nations also began funneling arms and money to the guerilla fighters. The American CIA employed Operation Cyclone to send arms to the Mujahideen. Foreign fighters that would later become the core of al-Qaeda also traveled to join the native Afghans against the Soviets.

By the spring of 1985, the Soviets hoped to begin transferring the burden of national defense to the Afghan army. The Russians attempted to build up the native forces. Although the official number of troops grew, the reality was that the force was riddled with desertion and disloyalty. In 1985, when Mikhail Gorbachev came to power in the USSR, Soviet policy changed dramatically. Many of these changes, which will be discussed in the next section, influenced the Soviet's policy in Afghanistan. When the Soviet Union finally left Afghanistan, over 600,000 of its service members had served in the country. The Soviet forces suffered over 14,000 casualties. This number does not reflect the high number of soldiers who suffered from illness or injury, many of whom were left with permanent disabilities.

The cost to the Afghan people was high as well. The true number of civilian casualties is unknown, but some estimates are as high as 1.5 million. This also does not reflect the millions of people who were displaced, and the damage done to the nation's infrastructure. The Soviet landmines planted during the war are still a hazard. The nearly decade-long conflict left one of the world's poorest countries even poorer. In the power vacuum left when the Soviets were gone, the nation fell into civil war, which only continued the suffering.

 Section 7: Reform and Collapse

SECTION 7.1: GLOBAL CHALLENGERS

As the Afghanistan conflict ended the season of détente that Russia had enjoyed in the 1970s, many world leaders stepped into place to challenge the Soviet status. *Détente* is a French word that means *relaxation*. It is commonly used to describe when a political situation becomes less tense. American leaders such as Richard Nixon and Gerald Ford had attempted to improve American relations with communist nations in the 1960s and 1970s. The desire to avoid nuclear conflict motivated this strategy.

This time period resulted in the negotiation and signature of different agreements such as the SALT treaties and the Helsinki Accords. SALT stood for Strategic Arms Limitation Talks. These agreements focused on limiting nuclear weapons and their delivery platforms. Though the U.S. had signed SALT I, the U.S. never ratified SALT II due to opposition to the Russian invasion of Afghanistan.

At the very end of the 1970s and the very beginning of the 1980s, new leaders came on the scene in the west. These leaders gained power in part due to the changes in globalization and the stagnation that had occurred in the western economies during the 1970s. In 1979, Margaret Thatcher became the prime minister of the United Kingdom. In the mid-1970s, Thatcher headed the Conservative Party, and she was the first woman to achieve this important role. She followed this success with election to the United Kingdom's top political office: prime minister. She filled her agenda with measures to help improve the lagging economy. Unemployment had been at a high, and she pushed for reforms that would deregulate many industries. The Russian invasion of Afghanistan occurred immediately after she took office as prime minister. Thatcher's opposition to communism would color the rest of her time in office. She would form a close relationship to the incoming president of the United States, Ronald Reagan, who held similar opinions of the communist state. Thatcher would collaborate closely with the U.S., including allowing Americans to station missiles on English soil.

Ronald Reagan succeeded Jimmy Carter as president of the United States in 1980. Reagan had formerly been an actor, and he brought a strong sense of charisma into the White House. As the president of the Screen Actors Guild—an influential Hollywood organization—he had worked to identify communists in the 1950s. Like Thatcher, he reacted to poor economic conditions in the United States. He emphasized tax cuts and deregulation. He also worked to reduce the high interest rates that had plagued the country.

Regarding foreign policy, Reagan aggressively increased American military spending. The president increased the number of personnel in the military, and he increased spending on both equipment and research and development to perfect new equipment. Reagan was counting on the communist economy not being able to handle the stress of keeping up with the American free market.

Both Reagan and Thatcher would condemn the communist ideology openly in famous speeches. In a speech in June of 1982, Reagan predicted that the socialist ideology would end up "on the ash heap of history." Another famous quote by Reagan came in March of 1983 when Reagan termed the USSR "an evil empire." Reagan was not scared to use events against the Soviet Union. He harshly condemned the USSR when the Soviet Union shot down a Korean Air Lines flight in 1983.

Reagan was prepared to commit more than just his speeches to opposing the Soviet Union. Under the Reagan Doctrine, the United States would send aid to anti-communist groups all over the globe. These efforts took place in Asia, Latin America, and

Africa. These operations were responsible for arming the Mujahideen against the Soviet invaders in Afghanistan.

On top of all his other strategies, Reagan introduced a new concept that left the Soviet Union scrambling to keep up. The Strategic Defense Initiative was a plan that was designed to integrate ground and space capabilities to defeat nuclear missiles that might be launched by the Soviet Union. While Reagan applauded the Strategic Defense Initiative and asserted that it would virtually negate Russian nuclear capabilities, some critics thought that the initiative was not possible. Whether or not the initiative was possible, leading Soviets believed that the initiative weakened the Soviet Union's ability to strike the U.S.

Despite Reagan's aggressive stance toward the Soviet Union, the president enjoyed overwhelming support from the American public and won a second term in office in 1984. Reagan began putting pressure on the new Russian leader, Mikhail Gorbachev, in the latter part of the 1980s, and the two would meet for several summits throughout the president's second term. Reagan never wavered from his message. He continually criticized the communist system and called for more liberties for the people behind the Iron Curtain.

Pope John Paul II was a third leader who influenced the Soviet Union. A pope of Polish descent, John Paul II was especially sensitive to the plight of his people locked behind the Iron Curtain. The pope had experienced the harsh rule of the Nazis and the Soviets. Pope John Paul II would not veil his disapproval of the Soviet Union, both because of its endorsement of atheism and because of its denial of human rights to its people.

The Polish Solidarity movement, which opposed the communist regime, took courage from the election of the new pope. The Poles were not the only ones interested in a Polish pope. Yuri Andropov, the head of the KGB, also realized that a pope of Polish descent could stir up opposition in Eastern Europe.

The pope published *Redemptor Hominis*, which emphasized the major themes of his messages. The pope would repeat a very basic message many times, that a curtailment of religious freedom was an attack on the dignity of a human being. The pope condemned societies where the faithful were persecuted and denied citizenship.

John Paul II was able to visit his homeland in 1979. He preached to the Polish people, condemning the totalitarian regime through his message of human dignity. Millions of people came to hear him speak. At one point, the pope carried a large wooden cross, and many people interpreted the cross as representing the communist burden on the Polish people. At times, the crowds chanted, "We want God." The communist community was scared by the implications of the pope's message and the people's reactions. An assassin, possibly hired at the direction of the Soviet secret police, attempted to kill the pope. Miraculously, the pope survived and continued preaching his message of human rights and religious freedom throughout the world.

SECTION 7.2: EXTERNAL FACTORS (AFGHANISTAN, ISLAM)

Of the fifteen socialist states that made up the Soviet Union after 1922, nearly half of those states were nations that had a Muslim majority. Azerbaijan, Kazakhstan, Kirghizia (now known as Kyrgyzstan), Tajikistan, Turkmenistan, and Uzbekistan all shared large Muslim populations. While the Soviet government discouraged and persecuted those choosing to practice the religion, the Muslim heritage was still evident in those regions. The Russian attack on Afghanistan only furthered the growth of the radical view of Islam. While the Soviet authorities burned books and closed mosques, the religious education system merely went underground. As the more moderate believers acquiesced to the regime, the radical adherents gathered followers. When Stalin allowed religious freedom to briefly return during World War II, the Muslim leaders who remained were of the radical sort. These leaders had the foresight to strategically emplace their followers into positions of authority in their regions. As there was another thaw into the 1970s, the radical beliefs were being passed through a network of tea houses and other informal gathering places.

As Russia entered the 1980s, it further alienated the Muslim population with the brutal invasion and treatment of Afghanistan. The war in Afghanistan combined with other factors, and the 1980s saw a liberalization of the policies that had prevented travel in earlier decades. Now the peoples in the mostly Muslim countries received more access to outside information and were already predisposed to radical religious views. The religious leaders were poised and organized at the fall of the Soviet empire to replace the old regime with leaders. These new governments were much more amenable to the religious views of the radicalized population.

SECTION 7.3: PERESTROIKA AND GLASNOST

Brezhnev did not enjoy good health toward the end of his time in office. Throughout the years of 1981 and 1982, several leaders stepped in to run the country while Brezhnev struggled with various ailments. The key figures during this time were Andrei Gromyko, Dmitriy Ustinov, Mikhail Suslov, and Yuri Andropov. While Suslov would have been a candidate to take Brezhnev's place, Suslov preceded the leader in death. Andropov, the head of the KGB, became the candidate vying for the leadership position. Andropov even began a campaign of rumors to discredit the still-living Brezhnev, accusing the dying statesman of corruption.

Brezhnev refused to hand over power, even as he suffered strokes. On November 7, 1982, the leader viewed the annual parade celebrating the October Revolution. Three days later, he died of a heart attack. Having ruled the USSR longer than any other leader besides Stalin, Brezhnev left a mixed legacy. He had tried to improve the nation's standard of living, but his adherence to communist ideology had also assured the economy's stagnation in the mid-1970s, coinciding with global economic difficulties. His lack of creativity with regard to solving economic policies would lessen his reputation. The other large stain on his legacy would be his nation's involvement in Afghanistan. However, he had been a stable leader. His time in office had seen a time of détente, and he had helped his nation finally catch up with the rest of world in many key areas. Russia could actually be said to have recovered from the decimation of World War II under his leadership.

Andropov, who had served as the chairman of the KGB longer than any other leader, took power after Brezhnev's death. The western nations were suspicious of Andropov because of the fact that he had led the KGB for so long. Immediately, the differences of style between the old leader and the new one became apparent: where Brezhnev had sought cohesion, Andropov was not afraid of conflict. Andropov sought to expose to the public the corruption or failure of leaders who had not made choices beneficial to the economy. In regard to foreign policy, Andropov did explore an exit from Afghanistan. He also faced Reagan's "evil empire" comment and the American Strategic Defense Initiative. Andropov would succumb to kidney failure and a host of other ailments in 1984, and Konstantin Chernenko, his successor, died of similar ailments in 1985.

Promoted by Andropov to a more powerful position, Mikhail Gorbachev assumed control of the Soviet Union in March of 1985. Significantly, Gorbachev would be the first and last leader of the Soviet Union born after the October Revolution. His priority was the economy. While announcing a vague agenda at the beginning of his entrance into office, he soon began to realize that the lack of economic growth stemmed from structural problems in the political and social systems of his country.

Gorbachev began actively advocating for radical changes in May 1985. Gorbachev embarked on making controversial changes. He replaced the Minister of Foreign Affairs, Andrei Gromyko, with Eduard Shevardnadze. This was a radical change because Gromyko had served in that position for almost three decades. Gorbachev was also willing to take on social ills that had been more or less accepted under previous Russian leaders. Gorbachev took on the Russian problem with alcoholism. While he seemed to be taking the nation in a new direction, he tried to assure the leadership that socialism was still the predominant force.

Gorbachev soon fleshed out his idea. *Perestroika*, the Russian word for *restructuring*, became the term Gorbachev adopted for his reforms. Many experts would credit perestroika with ending the Cold War. In the February and March 1986 Congress, Gorbachev tried to describe the actions that would usher in a new era of Soviet policy to renew the economy. While he described broad, sweeping concepts, he did not give many specifics. While perestroika was meant to reform, it was only meant for economic reforms and nothing more. More specifics would be forthcoming in 1987. Gorbachev proposed things like elections involving more than one candidate. He also proposed that non-communist party members should be allowed more participation in the economy. Before, only party members had enjoyed choice jobs. Gorbachev even published a book titled *Perestroika: New Thinking for Our Country and the World*.

Much of the substance of perestroika was introduced in the summer of 1987 when the Supreme Soviet of the Soviet Union enacted a law on state enterprise. For the first time, state industries were allowed to determine what they would produce based more on consumer demand. While the state enterprise still had to cover state orders first, they had more freedom to determine production. There was also more flexibility introduced to allow unprofitable enterprises to discontinue production. Enterprises had to bear responsibility for making enough money to cover their expenses. The plan also tried to shift power from ministries to the workers' collectives. Perhaps the most daring part of the plan was to allow foreign investors to partner with various government entities in the form of a joint venture.

Despite these reforms, the economy did not improve. Although Gorbachev had intended for many unprofitable portions of the economy to die off, the government continued to pay. More local governments withheld tax revenue from the central government because they felt more empowered. Lastly, although a central authority no longer mandated the production of consumer goods, no system replaced the command economy. The Russian economy could not figure out how to gauge consumer needs, and the consumer faced the same problems they had always faced in relation to consumer goods.

While the western nations watched the Soviet economy flounder, their economies were booming. The 1980s and 1990s were a time of unprecedented growth in the United States. However, the United States was very conservative in its approach toward Russia. The Americans did not send aid to the Russians, viewing their regime as incompatible with U.S. values.

Gorbachev additionally brought the term *demokratizatsiya* to the Russian consciousness. Gorbachev advocated for reforms that would diversify the political landscape of the Soviet Union. Beginning in 1987, Gorbachev would intentionally challenge the one-party system. The policy of *demokratizatsiya* would not have worked without another Gorbachev initiative—*glasnost*.

Gorbachev also instituted another radical policy known as *glasnost*. He tried to reform the government so that there would be more transparency. This Russian word refers to a concept where the state is more open with its people. In essence, Gorbachev was trying to conduct more of the government's affairs in the open. The leader wanted to encourage discussion of the nation's problems with the hope that solutions would appear.

The largest change under glasnost was a slight relaxation of freedom of speech after the government had controlled the press for decades. The media enjoyed slightly more freedom to critique the government. While Gorbachev hoped that this openness would lead to some reforms, the openness actually stirred up more opposition against the government. Unlike Gorbachev had hoped, the more people were able to voice their opinions, the more they sided entirely against the government.

For the first time, the media could be more honest when reporting about social problems. Before glasnost, the media had to avoid any coverage that would point out the shortcomings of the government. Faced with the truth about housing and food issues, as well as other basic societal issues such as the treatment of women and the rampant alcoholism in the Russian culture, people became disillusioned with a government that had seemingly lied to them for years. As more information passed between Russia and the outside world, the Soviet people soon realized that they enjoyed a far lower standard of living than people in the western world, despite their country's scientific and military achievements. For the people who had been true believers in socialism, this was especially bitter. They wondered what other lies the government had told them.

The Chernobyl nuclear reactor disaster would symbolize the problems inherent in the communist nation. Located in northern Ukraine, the Chernobyl nuclear disaster would scar a fertile region of Ukrainian land. The disaster would also negatively impact the entire nation as the plant was located on the Dnieper River, a river than ran directly through Ukraine's capital, Kiev. Chernobyl Nuclear Power Plant was located near the town of Pripyat in the very northern part of Ukraine. While the plant had been operating for several years, key safety precautions had only been tested. Certain safety features had never had a successful test.

These crucial safety measures, designed to run water through turbines in order to cool the reactor, had never worked in the previous tests occurring in 1982, 1984, and 1985. Many factors combined during April 26, 1986, resulting in a disaster. The previous day shift had been aware of the proposed test, but after several delays, they departed before the test was complete. Also, key officials were never informed about the test.

Many important safety features had been bypassed in order for the test to take place. While trying to power down the core, the power increased. The power increase resulted in an explosion at the nuclear core. The reactor, lacking any containment shell, expelled massive amounts of radioactivity. The resulting fire from the explosion made the radioactive dispersion worse. As the explosion rained debris onto the adjoining structures, including other reactors, the other structures faced fire. The situation was critical as personnel were struggling to maintain safe operations in the other reactors and fight fires. Many of the personnel who were on site received deadly doses of radiation within minutes. The firefighters who responded to the disaster were not told that the nuclear explosion had caused the fire. They initially believed that the fire's source was merely an electrical malfunction.

None of the firefighters and few to none of the personnel working on the site had proper equipment to deal with the radioactivity. Even if they had been told about the high levels of radiation, it is unlikely that any equipment could have protected them from the extreme levels of radiation that were produced in certain parts of the plant. As the firefighters raced to extinguish fires before the cooling systems of the other reactors were damaged, they received lethal doses of radiation. With the help of helicopters dropping materiel to suppress the fires, the crews were able to reduce the threat to the other reactors.

Pripyat, only a short distance away, was not informed of the accident. Soon, residents began suffering from acute radiation poisoning. Along with the residents of Pripyat, the leaders of Ukraine were also ignorant of the accident. Moscow owned the facility, and Moscow simply did not inform anyone in the Ukrainian government that anything more serious than a small fire had occurred.

Within twenty-four hours, at least two individuals had died from radiation poisoning, and Soviet officials flew in to investigate the accident site. On April 27, officials decided to evacuate the nearby town. They did not believe that the evacuation would be for long; however, the evacuation footprint would grow to permanently include evacuation of a radius of nineteen miles around the plant. The people, not anticipating a permanent removal, left their homes with few to no personal belongings with them. The outside world began ascertaining the scope of the accident long before the Soviet government would inform its own people. Swedish officials detected radiation and realized that it had originated within the Soviet Union. The Soviet media made a short announcement two days after the accident had occurred, not giving any indication of the magnitude of the destruction.

The plant's materials were volatile, and the government had to conceive a plan to contain the building. Using over 2,500 construction workers because of the desire to limit each individual's exposure to the radiation, engineers employed concrete to trap the remaining contaminants. The reactor was sealed off in a massive concrete sarcophagus. The efforts to contain the remaining nuclear material in its concrete shell finished in December 1986. The workers who erected the concrete suffered from radiation levels that often exceeded any safety standards. The government rewarded their efforts with special medals, created especially for the Chernobyl clean up.

After the accident, the vast majority of the contamination traveled to Belarus, adjoining the northern part of Ukraine. Within the first ninety days of the disaster, thirty-one people had died from the acute radiation poisoning while over 200 had acute radiation poisoning. Another effect of the radiation was a high incidence of thyroid cancer in children.

While the human toll does not seem overwhelming, the accident took a large toll in other areas. Financially, the disaster inflicted a huge cost on the flagging Russian economy. The cost of containment and decontamination was around $18 billion in 1986 dollars. Governments in the region, especially Ukraine and Belarus, are still spending relatively high percentages of their budget on expenses related to the disaster.

Politically, this disaster meant that Gorbachev would implement his glasnost policy to inform the United States of the disaster with the hopes that the U.S. would share knowledge. The disaster also deepened the distrust that the Soviet people had for their own government. Many felt betrayed by the way that the government had delayed the evacuation of the surrounding population. Ironically, the plant had continued operating despite the disaster. The last reactor at the site operated until the year 2000 because Ukraine had trouble providing energy to its people.

Gorbachev officially ushered in the era of glasnost in 1988. Incidents like Chernobyl and the new policy of glasnost gave Eastern Bloc countries a voice to raise concerns about their environments. Individuals began enjoying freedom of speech, and the media had more freedom to publish what it wanted to publish. To communist hardliners within the government, the strategy did not succeed as he intended. Gorbachev had wanted more debate and support of his proposed economic measures. The people did not choose to side exclusively with him.

In May of 1988, Gorbachev's policies dramatically challenged the conservative socialist dogma. Gorbachev formulated the Law on Cooperatives, which allowed for massive changes to the economic system. This law openly permitted free market activities such as private ownership of businesses in certain sectors. This kind of private ownership had not been seen in the Soviet Union since Lenin had permitted private ownership under the New Economic Plan. Although the law did penalize private ownership to some extent—through higher taxes and employment laws—many localities simply ignored these penalties. Later changes to the Law on Cooperatives even took away some of the restrictions and penalties. Additionally, these private businesses were allowed to solicit foreign investment.

The next month saw another radical change as Gorbachev tried to implement reforms that challenged the communist party's control of government systems. Gorbachev proposed a democratically elected legislative body called the Congress of People's Deputies. Free elections took place for the first time in the spring of 1989, and soon Gorbachev received a new title as the Chairman of the Supreme Soviet. The Russian people had not enjoyed such free participation in their political system since 1917.

The Deputies would soon vote on a leader, and Gorbachev, as the only candidate on the ballot, received enough votes to become the president of the Soviet Union. Although Gorbachev had more or less been responsible for the liberalization of the government and the new freely elected legislature, he also received the brunt of the criticism that was now more open than ever before. The Congress was able to air its debate in Soviet news media. People were aware of the workings of their government and began to expect faster and more dramatic changes to the structure of their government and economy. Gorbachev's grip on power in his country began to weaken, despite the fact that he had been responsible for many of the reforms.

Where glasnost worked, in the sense that the Russian people began to enjoy concrete benefits from this policy, perestroika did not. The openness permitted under glasnost merely allowed the failures of perestroika to face stronger criticism. The conservative and hardliner communists never quite allowed perestroika to completely enact the change that the economy needed. In the western economies, economic policy catered toward a larger population: the voter. In the old Soviet system, the economic policy traditionally favored a much smaller population: the party member. In the short term, the changes of perestroika would have only caused more difficulties for the party members. The communist leaders would have lost their access to their economic privileges while the rest of Soviet population caught up. In addition, there would have been price increases and labor shifts as the economy adjusted to the demand of the consumer rather than to the command of the central planner. The hardliners blocked changes at every turn because they had the most to lose in the short term under this economic reform. The hardliners were never willing to let go of the system that crippled the Russian economy and benefitted them.

Gorbachev's reforms reflected only halfhearted changes. Fixed prices remained in place, hampering economic growth. While Gorbachev's policies would help to end the USSR, he did not want that to be the result. Even years after his departure from Russian office, Gorbachev criticized free market economies. When the housing bubble in the United States caused tremendous economic difficulties around 2008 and 2009, Gorbachev used that opportunity to criticize the free market. He also opined that the free market robs its people of a safety net that the people in socialist countries enjoy. Gorbachev's reforms had been an attempt to save the communist party, not end it. He intended his reforms to enable the communist system to adapt to changing times. He did not envision that the reforms would enable the people to change the political system. Some of Gorbachev's fears materialized as Russia rejected the communist party completely by 1991. There was chaos in the economy, and the transition was not easy or smooth, as will be discussed below.

Glasnost also brought mixed consequences to the communist regime. Gorbachev had intended that glasnost bring about criticism of the old system so that reforms would be accepted. Of course, this was meant to reform the communist system and not replace it. Glasnost was at once criticized by the hardliners and exploited by those who wanted change. While Gorbachev wanted the regime to stay in place, the people began questioning his motives and became aware of how many lies their government had told them. As criticism of the harsh leaders like Stalin and Brezhnev trickled down into society, Russian history books revealed themselves to be laughably inaccurate. The Russian people were appalled, not only by the deeds of their former leaders, but also the treatment of the land. Glasnost forced the Russian government to expose their failures after the Chernobyl disaster. The truth about the Chernobyl disaster led to revelations about other environmental problems. The Russian people were angered by how central planners had squandered and abused the natural resources. The policy of glasnost contributed to the government's embarrassment.

Although Gorbachev's policies were not a clear success at home, he enjoyed a growing respect among the western powers that recognized that he was changing many of the aspects of the communist government that the west had ideologically opposed. Gorbachev's cultivation of relationships outside of Russia did give the nation leeway to allocate some of its money toward non-military spending, thus slowing the arms race. Gorbachev was tirelessly working to build personal relationships with the leaders of the western world. He cultivated relationships with Margaret Thatcher, Ronald Reagan, and Helmut Kohl, the West German chancellor. From the spring of 1985, Gorbachev openly planned to cut defense programs, and he encouraged other western leaders to do the same. A crucial meeting in 1986 in Reykjavik between Gorbachev and Ronald Reagan led to an unprecedented agreement to remove both sides' intermediate range nuclear weapons from Europe. Gorbachev followed this agreement with another move that would gain the approval of the western leaders. Gorbachev made the decision to withdraw completely from Afghanistan in 1988. The war in Afghanistan had been unpopular among the worldwide community to start with, and now the free world applauded Gorbachev's policy.

Seeing the changes in the Soviet leadership, many political leaders began leveraging their influence. On June 12, 1987, Ronald Reagan visited the Brandenburg Gate in Berlin. The visit took place to celebrate Berlin's 750th anniversary. Standing within sight of the Berlin Wall, which had become a symbol of the oppressive Soviet regime, Ronald Reagan issued a direct challenge to Mikhail Gorbachev, the leader of the USSR. In a speech that would echo across the world, President Reagan said, "Mr. Gorbachev, tear down this wall!"

Soviet policy began to soften its grip on the Eastern Bloc nations. Shortly after Reagan's speech, another large policy shift gained the outside world's approval. Gorbachev soon dismantled the Brezhnev Doctrine. Leonid Brezhnev had enunciated policy that would become known as the Brezhnev Doctrine in 1968. In a speech justifying the invasion of Czechoslovakia, Brezhnev had announced that where anti-socialist forces were challenging the regime in one socialist country, this problem became the concern of all the other socialist countries. In essence, Brezhnev was communicating that any attempt by an Eastern Bloc country to break from the USSR sphere of influence would be stifled by the USSR.

Contradicting the Brezhnev policy, Gorbachev announced that Eastern Bloc nations would be free to govern their own affairs. Shockingly, Gorbachev even announced this policy in a speech before the Council of Europe on July 6, 1989. The momentous policy shifts earned Gorbachev favorable treatment from the western leaders as the 1980s ended and the 1990s began.

SECTION 7.4: REEMERGENCE OF THE NATIONALITIES ISSUE

For much of the Soviet Union's history, the regime had repressed nationalities through policies of Russification. At first, the Marxist government had attempted to build individual socialist nations out of the different ethnicities. In the 1926 census of the USSR, sixty-nine major nationalities were split among forty-five different bordered regions. At first, the government had attempted to help each region or territory create its own autonomous government with its own institutions and culture under the communist umbrella. However, coinciding with Stalin's repression, these efforts ceased around the mid-1930s. In the mid-1930s, Stalin became suspicious of non-Russian ethnicities.

Stalin's suspicion of everyone discouraged ethnic practices and cohesion. Through Stalin's time, and continuing after his death, the government began a campaign of Russification. Russian culture and language was exported to the non-Russian communities. Local expressions of culture and language faced repression. In the 1950s, Khrushchev actively replaced schools that had taught in ethnic languages with schools that taught in Russian. Over the course of the Soviet Union, schools taught fewer and fewer languages represented by the different ethnicities in the Soviet Union. Many children in the Soviet Union did not receive instruction in their native languages. Russian language instruction also helped cement the political structure of the Soviet Union and empower the communist party. The communist party recognized that ethnicities were as much a barrier to socialism as class distinctions. The use of Russian in government justified the instruction of Russian in schools. The instruction tried to draw the nationalities together.

When judging the nationalism that began to assert itself toward the end of the Soviet Union, it is also important to differentiate between different levels or forms of nationalism. Some of the nationalities that began to rally together had been sovereign nations before the Soviet Union swallowed their autonomy. The Baltic states of Estonia, Latvia, and Lithuania had enjoyed sovereignty as individual nations before World War II, and it was easy for their individual nationalism to surge as glasnost opened the Soviet Union to criticism. Some nationalism was based in larger part on common religious beliefs. Territories with large Muslim populations shared culture and values that directly opposed communist ideology, and these religious values united people against the Soviet Union.

However, assimilating the hundreds, if not thousands, of ethnicities represented in the Soviet Union was a monumental task. The task was nowhere near complete as Gorbachev began instituting his new policies in the 1980s. By 1986, the first signs of the fragmentation of the Soviet Union began to appear. Gorbachev replaced an ethnic Kazakh, Dinmukhamed Kunayev, with a non-ethnic Kazakh. The people of Kazakhstan protested the removal of the leader who had led the country for decades. On December 17, 1986, students gathered in the capital of Kazakhstan to protest the replacement. Although there is debate as to whether the protests were truly inspired by nationalism, there doubtless was an element of nationalism to the protests. In the end, the Soviet Union did not tolerate the protests and conflict broke out. The number of casualties is in dispute. Estimates range from two dead to a thousand. However, all reports agree that protesters died as a result of opposing the designated Soviet leader, and many were sentenced to forced labor.

With the growth of glasnost, leaders from the Baltic States begin to openly question the Soviet dogma. The Soviet Union maintained for decades that it was operating with the un-coerced consent of the nationalities. The local leaders became very vocal in their questioning of their nation's "consent."

At the end of the 1980s, it seemed as though each nationality was reacting in a different way against the Soviet central authority. In countries such as Georgia, Soviet soldiers would kill demonstrators who were demanding Georgian independence. In a different response, as Gorbachev tried to remove bad communist leaders from Central Asian areas, the local people were angered by the removal of leaders who shared their ethnicity, even though these leaders were corrupt and ineffective. Some regions, like Ukraine, saw a conflict among the people, some of whom had assimilated comfortably into the larger Russian culture and some of whom wanted a distinct Ukrainian nation. Thus, just like the ethnicities themselves, the era of glasnost elicited diverse responses among the different groups that had been sheltered under the USSR's umbrella. One thing united all movements: dissatisfaction with the status quo. Gorbachev's already difficult job only got more difficult as he juggled increased local tensions, which often resulted in clashes between his soldiers and the local people.

Violence occurred as demonstrations became commonplace. In May 1987, ethnic Russians protested in Moscow. Violence and protests broke out in Armenian enclaves in Azerbaijan, leading to a war. In 1988, with the situation made worse by a devastating earthquake, violence broke out between soldiers and protesters in Armenia. The elections that took place in 1989 only worsened the situation as communist party candidates faced defeat, and countries favored nationalist candidates. The television played a vital role in the growth of national movements. As nationalist views received coverage on television under the policy of glasnost, the ideas spread rapidly. In 1989, many nations, with the Baltic States leading the way, enacted legislation that gave their local languages preference over Russian. The tension grew between the Soviets and their satellites. On April 9, 1989, Soviet troops reacted to protests in Georgia, firing on the local people. Another incident in Uzbekistan in June resulted in deaths when soldiers fired on locals.

SECTION 7.5: REVOLUTIONS IN EASTERN EUROPE

On November 16, 1988, Estonia became the first country to break from the Eastern Bloc in a concrete way. It declared its sovereignty and adopted laws that ensured its local laws would be respected over the laws of the Soviet Union. By the summer of 1989, the other two Baltic States, Lithuania and Latvia, did the same thing. 1989 also brought an acknowledgement of what the Baltic States had suspected all along. Gorbachev released information to the public about the nature of the Molotov-Ribbentrop Pact and how it had planned to allow the Soviet Union to absorb the countries. While the countries were excited to find out the details of the dirty deal between Hitler and Stalin, they were also watching to find out whether Gorbachev would attempt to use the Soviet military to bring the countries back into the fold. The fiftieth anniversary of the Molotov-Ribbentrop Pact saw an upsurge in nationalism and protests. One of these famous protests occurred on August 23, 1989. Over two million citizens of the Baltic States joined hands to form a human chain across the countries of Estonia, Latvia, and Lithuania. This chain protested the Soviet's incorporation of the countries into the USSR. All were relieved when Gorbachev made no move to insert the Soviet military into the mix.

In Poland, a growing movement, known as Solidarity, opposed Soviet occupation. Solidarity was inspired by supporters of the Catholic Church. The Solidarity movement was led by Lech Walesa, who helped to organize the strikes that eventually forced communist leaders to engage in formal talks with the organization. The communist leadership eventually caved to the demands of the people and legalized the movement. Free elections took place in Poland on June 4, 1989. Communist party candidates did not achieve enough votes to take any seats. For the first time in decades, a Soviet Bloc nation had thrown off the communist party's domination. Walesa's inauguration on December 21, 1990 was the end of the People's Republic of Poland.

Hungary experienced a revolution as well. Hungary's parliament passed laws of their own formulation, and on January 29, 1989, the Hungarian government officially corrected history. No longer would the people be told that the 1956 Hungarian rebellion had been instigated by foreign powers. The truth could be told: there had been a popular uprising against the communist occupiers. Significantly, Hungary began removing the physical symbols of the Iron Curtain. The wall separating Hungary from Austria was destroyed. As Hungary opened its borders, citizens in other Eastern Bloc countries began using the border as a means of escape. Citizens from Czechoslovakia and the German Democratic Republic traveled to Hungary to exit the Eastern Bloc. Symbolically, the Hungarian leader, Imre Nagy, who had been executed by the Soviets in 1956, received a funeral in Budapest on June 16, 1989.

The ongoing opening of Hungary caused a massive exodus of people from the German Democratic Republic. Thousands tried to leave the communist nation. As the authorities attempted to close its borders, demonstrations began. Demonstrators anticipated violent repression on October 9, 1989. The leaders at the location of the protests refused to follow any order to fire on the protesters. As protests grew, the communist German leadership expected Russian aid, but none appeared. Hundreds of thousands of Germans began protesting the wall. By November 4, 1989, over half a million people gathered in protest in the main square of East Berlin, Alexanderplatz. Unable to respond in a timely or coordinated manner to the protests, one leader accidentally announced that the borders between the two parts of the city would be opened. As the sound bite looped through the news media, the people believed that the borders would be opened immediately and began assembling at checkpoints, demanding that the guards open the gates. As the crowds grew, and authorities were unwilling to give orders for guards to use force, the Berline residents stormed the wall. People spontaneously gathered, disassembling parts of the wall and creating their own access points.

The fall of the Berlin Wall would signal a free exchange of people between East and West Berlin. It would also bring about renewed plans for reunification, and the official destruction of the Berlin Wall began on June 13, 1990, with all roads between the two parts of the city becoming passable by August of 1990. By October 3, 1990, East Germany no longer existed, and in place of two countries, one unified Germany emerged, organized as a democratic country. The Soviet Union agreed with this course of action based on a negotiation of certain limitations on the unified Germany. Germany could enter NATO so long as their army would stay under 370,000 personnel and the country would not maintain any chemical, biological, or nuclear weapons in its arsenal.

As the Soviet military made no move to enter the Baltic States, nationalist forces swept through other regions under the Soviet sphere of influence. Anti-Soviet demonstrations broke out in Azerbaijan and Moldova. Armenia also tested the Soviet Union by trying to assert its veto right over laws directed by the Soviet Union. Azerbaijan tried to cope with the chaos by enacting legislation to favor its local laws over Soviet laws.

The Soviet army did try to intervene in Georgia. Thousands of Georgians had marched on the country's communist party headquarters. On April 7, 1989, the Red Army responded militarily. Two days later on April 9, 1989, the troops opened fire on protesters. As a result of the military intervention, twenty protesters died and hundreds were injured. This massacre turned the people against the Soviet leaders. Gorbachev moved to replace Georgia's leader; however, the region was descending into nationalist chaos.

In Ukraine, many protests stemmed from the condition of the nation's religious community. People held impromptu religious services and hunger strikes to draw attention to injustice. The year of 1989 brought recurrent protests by thousands of people, changes in leadership, and introduction of multi-party politics in the nation. It also brought a resurgence in the role of the church. The Ukrainian Autocephalous Orthodox Church held its first synod (assembly) since the 1930s. The people were uniting against the USSR's centralized rule.

Politically, it was significant that in the spring of 1990, the government changed Article 6 of the constitution. Prior to this time, Article 6 of the USSR's constitution had called for the communist party's monopoly of the political system. Thus, the regions were advocating for more autonomy, and at the same time, the government was setting the stage for more division in the ruling class. Article 6 of the USSR's constitution ensured that the communist party of the Soviet Union was the supreme organization in the Soviet Union. Gorbachev did not necessarily want to dismantle the communist party, but he also wanted to dis-empower the hardliners who were blocking reforms. Gorbachev hoped that in repealing Article 6, he would find allies in the more liberal wings of the government. Gorbachev convinced the Central Committee plenum to repeal Article 6 in February 1990. In addition to dismantling the communist party's power, Gorbachev also pushed to change the highest office of the Soviet Union. Gorbachev reorganized the top position in the Soviet Union, calling for the position to be elected by the People's Deputies and changing the name of the position to president. With the changes made, Gorbachev became the president of the USSR on March 15, 1990.

By the time Gorbachev assumed the new title of "president," fundamental changes were taking place all throughout the Soviet sphere of influence. Lithuania was the first country to openly declare its independence. On March 11, Lithuania declared its freedom from the Union of Soviet Socialist Republics. On March 30, 1990, Estonia passed legislation that condemned the Russian interference in the country to be illegal. Latvia followed suit on May 4, 1990.

Significantly, in January 1990, the Soviet Union was also losing control of its external borders with other countries. The Soviet Azerbaijanis stormed the border between the USSR and Iran and united with their relatives on the other side of the border. While the border was breaking down, violence was also increasing between ethnicities in the region, and Soviet troops were caught in the middle. With violence on all sides, communist hardliners tried to control the situation with the force of the Soviet army.

By October of 1990, the USSR was enveloped in chaos both inside and outside its borders. Ukraine and Russia moved to establish their own laws as taking precedence over the USSR's laws. Trying to assert his power over the situation, Gorbachev issued an ultimatum to Lithuania in 1991. On January 10, 1991, Gorbachev demanded that Lithuania accept the Soviet Union's constitution as valid and repeal all their national laws that asserted the predominance of Lithuanian laws. The KGB and other Russian agencies took action against the Lithuanian government, causing violence in the city of Vilnius. Gorbachev was slow to condemn the KGB's action at first, but eventually he began to concede that Lithuania could secede from the USSR if they did so according to the guidance of the USSR's constitution. While Gorbachev attempted to organize an orderly withdrawal of Soviet influence over the Eastern Bloc, Boris Yeltsin was elected as the new president of the Russian Federation in the summer of 1991, and the Warsaw Pact would end on July 1, 1991.

SECTION 7.6: END OF THE UNION OF SOVIET SOCIALIST REPUBLICS

The election of Boris Yeltsin marked the beginning of the end for the Soviet Union. Hardliners, opposing the Gorbachev-proposed treaty with the satellite nations, attempted a coup. Gennady Yanayev, the vice president, placed Gorbachev under house arrest in the Crimea, while he tried to reverse course. The coup lasted three days before Gorbachev was allowed to leave the dacha. While Gorbachev languished in the Crimea, Boris Yeltsin defied the coup leaders, which defeated the hardliners' momentum. Photos of Yeltsin reasoning with the coup leaders from atop a tank would become iconic of his role in the fall of the Soviet Union.

In the aftermath of Gorbachev's return, the leaders of the coup faced arrest for treason. A couple of the leaders killed themselves, and Gorbachev lost even more credibility in the eyes of his friends and enemies as the coup leaders had been close friends and associates of Gorbachev before the attempt to seize power.

Gorbachev held a title and no power after the coup. Boris Yeltsin did not answer to Gorbachev, and Gorbachev supervised the dissolution of the Central Committee. The Congress of People's Deputies also dissolved on September 5, 1991. By the end of 1991, the Union of Soviet Socialist Republics disappeared. From August 1991 until the end of the year, ten different republics fled the Soviet Union.

Ukraine, the most prosperous of the socialist republics, voted to secede from the USSR on December 1, 1991. Earlier in the year, the United States president, George H. W. Bush, had visited Ukraine and delivered a speech that would later be ridiculed as the "Chicken Kiev" speech. The heart of the speech was an appeal by the U.S. president for the Ukrainian people to give Gorbachev's policies a chance to work. The president was discouraging the Ukrainian people from asserting their independence. President Bush would later explain that he was not sure that the Soviet Union would peacefully allow the nation to secede. At the time, the Ukrainian parliament applauded the words. Ukrainian nationalists condemned the speech. Despite Bush's warning, over 90% of the people voted for independence.

On December 25, 1991, Gorbachev announced his resignation to the Russian people. The Soviet Union ceased to exist as of December 26, 1991, and in its place the Commonwealth of Independent States emerged. By December 8, 1991, Belarus, the Russian Federation, and Ukraine had entered into an agreement to create a successor organization to replace the USSR. The three countries formally opened the commonwealth to all the former Soviet republics. Since the nations would be deemed sovereign, the Soviet Union was officially dissolved since it was no longer the ultimate authority for the nations. Within weeks, by December 21, 1991, eight more countries joined: Armenia, Azerbaijan, Kazakhstan, Kyrgyzstan, Moldova, Turkmenistan, Tajikistan, and Uzbekistan. Georgia joined these first eleven countries in 1993, while Estonia, Latvia, and Lithuania refused to join.

SECTION 7.7: GORBACHEV'S LEGACY

Gorbachev has outlived most of the leaders of his era. Ronald Reagan and Margaret Thatcher have both died. As the populations who experienced his era of reforms from the mid-1980s to the early 1990s age, opinions soften. There is now some nostalgia toward the days of the Soviet Union. The Russian nation faced a difficult transition into the free market economy, and the standard of living for the average Russian did not improve as rapidly as the people had hoped. As polls question the aging population about their views of the Soviet Union, more are reporting favorable views of the regime than ever before.

However, Gorbachev's legacy is mixed. In the eyes of some, he was a visionary reformer. He was willing to undertake reforms that other leaders had been unwilling to attempt. He had presided over an era of increased freedom, and his reforms led to the eventual freeing of the Eastern Bloc nations from the Soviet sphere of influence. This mixed view of Gorbachev is represented by the reactions to Gorbachev's eightieth birthday. While Gorbachev enjoyed lavish treatment at a birthday celebration held in his honor in England, few in Russia noted the celebration.

Gorbachev likely never intended to be the reformer who brought an end to the Soviet Union. He perhaps was less passionate about change than people realize. Perhaps he was only pointing out the obvious with his slogan, "We can't go on like this." Gorbachev promised restructuring and attacked alcoholism. Perestroika did not deliver on its promises, and the Russian culture did not appreciate Gorbachev's attack on its vices. While Gorbachev was willing to enact superficial changes, he either did not understand or did not enact enough changes in the economy for the people to benefit. While Gorbachev talked about restructuring, he held on fiercely to Marxism. Gorbachev's economic policies did not work and were contradicted by the ideology he chose to cling to. In the process, he alienated the communist hardliners and did not satisfy the radicals. He was left in the middle, with no supporters.

Perhaps Gorbachev's legacy fares better when viewing his foreign policy. Gorbachev abandoned the arms race and the Brezhnev Doctrine, giving countries the latitude they needed to leave the Soviet Union. However, maybe these moves that the west applauded were more accidental than visionary.

Gorbachev and his legacy will be mixed. He never stuck to the communist ideology enough to please the party, and he did not embrace reform either. Although he was responsible for hastening the end of the Soviet Union, it was not his intention. This is why Gorbachev is not popular among his own people as he did not really embrace a side. The outside world appreciates the fact that Gorbachev hastened the end of the Cold War, but for the Russian people, the end came either too fast or far too slow.

Sample Test Questions

1) _____ was a weak leader overall, and his inaction proved fatal for the Romanov Empire as he would be the last of the Romanov dynasty to reign.

   A) Tsar Alexander II
   B) Tsar Alexander III
   C) Tsar Nicholas II
   D) King George

The correct answer is C:) Tsar Nicholas II. Nicholas II began to lose touch with the affairs of his nation while he spent time trying to lead the effort against the Germans in World War I. While he spent time micromanaging military leaders, the tsarina and Rasputin damaged the reputation of the monarchy. Section 1.1.

2) _____ was responsible for freeing the serfs in 1861.

   A) Tsar Alexander II
   B) Tsar Alexander III
   C) Tsar Nicholas II
   D) King George

The correct answer is A:) Tsar Alexander II. Tsar Alexander II was a much more liberal leader than previous tsars. He enacted many economic and social reforms. Section 1.1.

3) Reversing the liberal policies of his father, _____ returned power to the monarchy, setting a course for more social unrest in Russia.

   A) Tsar Alexander II
   B) Tsar Alexander III
   C) Tsar Nicholas II
   D) King George

The correct answer is B:) Tsar Alexander III. Tsar Alexander III was deeply affected by his father's assassination, which occurred even though Tsar Alexander II had been a more liberal ruler. Section 1.1.

4) _____ was the finance minister who attempted to modernize industry and railways.

   A) Leo Tolstoy
   B) Peter Stolypin
   C) Sergei Witte
   D) Winston Churchill

The correct answer is C:) Sergei Witte. Witte attempted to attract foreign investors to Russia, bringing capital into the country. Section 1.2.

5) The time from Alexander II's assassination until 1905 could best be described as _____.

   A) Democratization
   B) Socialism
   C) Communism
   D) Russification

The correct answer is D:) Russification. In reaction to the more liberal Tsar Alexander II, the tsars that came after him reversed course and tried to homogenize the diverse nation through mandatory Russian language instruction and oppression of smaller ethnic groups. Section 1.1.

6) Russia's _____ played a large role in the nation's eventual defeat by the Japanese during the Russo-Japanese War.

   A) Support for the Chinese
   B) Underestimation of the Japanese
   C) Revolutionary leaders
   D) Outdated fleet

The correct answer is B:) Underestimation of the Japanese. Russia had a fairly modern fleet, but the Japanese had also modernized both their equipment and their tactics. Section 1.4.

7) _____ wrote the influential novel *What Is to Be Done?* which pointed toward socialism as the cure to Russia's woes.

   A) Maxim Gorky
   B) Vladimir Lenin
   C) Leon Trotsky
   D) Nikolai Chernyshevsky

The correct answer is D:) Nikolai Chernyshevsky. This novel inspired a wave of socialist writings, including Lenin's famous pamphlet, which shared the same name. Section 1.1.

8) _____ is considered the last statesman of tsarist Russia.

   A) Leo Tolstoy
   B) Peter Stolypin
   C) Sergei Witte
   D) Winston Churchill

The correct answer B:) Peter Stolypin. Stolypin had a systematic vision for Russian foreign and domestic policy. His bold approach resulted in his probably falling out of favor with Tsar Nicholas II; however, Stolypin died at the hands of an assassin before the tsar could remove him. Section 1.5.

9) After Lenin advocated for a radical socialist view that the proletariat could not achieve socialism on its own and would need to be directed by socialist leaders, the Russian Social Democratic Labor Party divided into two factions: _____.

   A) The Republicans and the Democrats
   B) The Bolsheviks and the Mensheviks
   C) The Socialists and the Communists
   D) The Anarchists and the Monarchists

The correct answer is B:) The Bolsheviks and the Mensheviks. Even though the Bolsheviks were actually in the numerical minority at their founding, Lenin took the name, which meant "member of the majority" in Russian, to describe his followers. Section 1.1.

10) Tsar Nicholas attempted to regain control over the nation by authoring the _____ in October 1905.

   A) October Manifesto
   B) Treaty of Portsmouth
   C) Emancipation Proclamation
   D) Communist Manifesto

The correct answer is A:) October Manifesto. The tsar wanted to appear as though he was giving into pressure to loosen his grip as an absolute monarch. The reforms set forth in the October Manifesto would be short-lived. Section 1.5.

11) The two most important authors of long prose works during the Golden Age of Literature in Russia were _____.

   A) Leo Tolstoy and Alexander Pushkin
   B) Leo Tolstoy and Fyodor Dostoyevsky
   C) Fyodor Dostoyevsky and Maxim Gorky
   D) Alexander Pushkin and Anton Chekhov

The correct answer is B:) Leo Tolstoy and Fyodor Dostoyevsky. Tolstoy and Dostoyevsky both treated the topics of poverty and morality in their epics. Section 1.3.

12) With Tsar Nicholas spending time away from St. Petersburg directing the Russian war efforts, _____ had more opportunity to direct domestic policy.

   A) The kulaks
   B) Rasputin and the tsarina
   C) Leo Tolstoy and Maxim Gorky
   D) Vladimir Lenin

The correct answer is B:) Rasputin and the tsarina. Many feared that the tsarina's dependence was discrediting the monarchy, and eventually motivated the killing of Rasputin. Section 2.1.

13) After World War I, Lenin instituted the _____ in order to allow the nation's economy to recover, and this strategy allowed for some vestiges of the free market to appear.

   A) New Deal
   B) Perestroika
   C) New Economic Policy
   D) Five Year Plan

The correct answer is C:) New Economic Policy. Stalin resoundingly rejected the New Economic Policy after Lenin's death. Section 2.5.

14) On _____ under the old calendar or _____ under the new calendar, Tsar Nicholas II abdicated the Russia throne.

   A) March 2, 1917, March 15, 1917
   B) May 11, 1917, May 24, 1917
   C) October 25, 1917, November 7, 1917
   D) June 10, 1918, July 8, 1918

The correct answer is A:) March 2, 1917, March 15, 1917. Section 2.1.

15) The Bolshevik Revolution occurred on _____ under the old calendar or _____ under the new calendar.

   A) March 2, 1917, March 15, 1917
   B) May 11, 1917, May 24, 1917
   C) October 25, 1917, November 7, 1917
   D) June 10, 1918, July 8, 1918

The correct answer is C:) October 25, 1917, November 7, 1917. Section 2.3.

16) _____ led the Bolsheviks, organizing the October Revolution.

A) Leon Trotsky
B) Vladimir Lenin
C) Lev Kamenev
D) Grigory Zinoviev

The correct answer is B:) Vladimir Lenin. Lenin had organized the October Revolution in accordance with his vision, presented earlier in the April Theses. Section 2.3.

17) _____ was another key leader in the Bolshevik movement, organizing the Bolshevik security forces and eventually the Red Army.

A) Leon Trotsky
B) Vladimir Lenin
C) Lev Kamenev
D) Grigory Zinoviev

The correct answer is A:) Leon Trotsky. Leon Trotsky would also be key in the treaty to end the Russian involvement in World War I. Section 2.3.

18) Appearing as _____ over the course of the USSR's history, the Russian secret police were even more repressive than they had been under the tsar.

A) CIA, FBI, and DOD
B) HDS, BDV, TRE, and SPE
C) Cheka, OGPU, NKVD, and NKGB
D) MIG, KGB, and KO.

The correct answer is C:) Cheka, OGPU, NKVD, and NKGB. Section 2.4.

19) _____ was a key battle for Russia in World War I and signaled the beginning of unsuccessful campaigns for the Russians as the German inflicted heavy casualties on them with the help of inept Russian commanders and knowledge of the Russian code.

A) The Battle of Stalingrad
B) The Battle of Leningrad
C) The Battle of Tannenberg
D) The Battle of Moscow

The correct answer is C:) The Battle of Tannenberg. Russia had fielded a force of 150,000 before the battle, and only 10,000 remained after the battle. Section 2.1.

20) Under the New Economic Policy, the urban population declined by _____.

    A) One-fourth
    B) One-third
    C) One-half
    D) One-eighth

The correct answer is C:) One-half. This erosion of the urban population would cause the communist leaders concern because the urban population had been much more supportive of the socialist agenda than the rural population. Section 2.5.

21) The _____ presented Lenin's view on how the Bolsheviks should proceed with a secondary revolution.

    A) April Theses
    B) Ninety-five Theses
    C) Testament
    D) October Manifesto

The correct answer is A:) April Theses. This work inspired his followers to take action to defeat the provisional government through strategic placement of socialist leaders and systematic use of propaganda. Section 2.3.

22) The Bolsheviks effectively disbanded the _____ through intimidation after the members had met for only a matter of hours between January 17 and 18, 1918.

    A) Soviet
    B) Duma
    C) Constituent Assembly
    D) Congress

The correct answer is C:) Constituent Assembly. The Bolsheviks had plans to disregard the Constituent Assembly when it became clear that they had not won the popular vote. The Bolsheviks attempted to legitimize their actions when the All-Russian Central Executive Committee also ratified the action to disband the Constituent Assembly. Section 2.3.

23) The _____ ended Russian involvement in World War I on March 3, 1918.

   A) Treaty of Portsmouth
   B) Molotov-Ribbentrop pact
   C) Pact of Paris
   D) Treaty of Brest-Litovsk

The correct answer is D:) Treaty of Brest-Litovsk. This treaty, negotiated by Trotsky, would seed large swathes of formerly Russian territory to its opponents. Section 2.3.

24) The predominant style of artwork in the Soviet Union, _____, focused on portraying scenes that would advance the ideals of socialism.

   A) Surrealism
   B) Dadaism
   C) Socialist realism
   D) Social realism

The correct answer is C:) Socialist realism. Unlike social realism which focused on the poor as a subject of pity, socialist realism adulates the common worker. Section 3.5.

25) Praised for his work *The Mother*, _____ helped define socialist realism in literature and created a novel in which the true hero was a woman who learned to embrace communist ideals.

   A) Maxim Gorky
   B) Leo Tolstoy
   C) Leon Trotsky
   D) Anna Akhmatova

The correct answer is A:) Maxim Gorky. The pseudonym literally meant Maxim the Bitter. Section 3.5.

26) The work of _____ is some of the best-known Russian poetry of the twentieth century. This author wrote both longer and shorter works that both criticized and praised Stalin.

   A) Anna Akhmatova
   B) Leo Tolstoy
   C) Andrei Zhdanov
   D) Mikhail Gorbachev

The correct answer is A:) Anna Akhmatova. This author was condemned by Andrei Zhdanov, who formulated the Russian cultural policy. Although she disliked Stalin, she wrote poems praising him as she was trying to have her son released from Stalin's labor camp. Section 3.5.

27) Stalin accused the _____ of hoarding their grain and being anti-revolutionary, leading to the collectivization of their land and their persecution as a class of people.

   A) Kulaks
   B) Jews
   C) Revolutionaries
   D) Trotskyists

The correct answer is A:) Kulaks. Kulak referred to the wealthier peasants who had been able to achieve some measure of economic success. Section 3.2.

28) An ethnic Georgian, _____ assumed control of the Soviet Union after Lenin's death.

   A) Josef Stalin
   B) Leon Trotsky
   C) Alexander Romanov
   D) Julius Martov

The correct answer is A:) Josef Stalin. Josef Stalin would centralize much of the power of the nation in himself, executing and exiling millions of his own population. Section 3.1.

29) The kulaks were independent farmers, but _____ were the collectively owned farming associations that were favored under Stalin.

   A) Sovkhozy
   B) Kolkhozy
   C) Commune
   D) Soviet

The correct answer is B:) Kolkhozy. Where kolkhozy indicated communal ownership, sovkhozy indicated state ownership. Section 3.2.

30) Stalin's centrally direct _____ became the standard in economic planning for the nation when he introduced his first in 1928.

   A) Budget
   B) New Economic Plan
   C) Dekulakization
   D) Five-Year Plan

The correct answer is D:) Five-Year Plan. If the state determined that the objectives of each five-year plan had been accomplished, the state might announce a new plan in less than five years. Section 3.2.

31) During the second five-year plan, a group of highly motivated workers named the _____ received credit for helping the industries meet their production goals.

   A) Soviet workers
   B) Kolkhozy
   C) Stakhanovite Movement
   D) Kulaks

The correct answer is C:) Stakhanovite Movement. The Stakhanovite Movement was named after a coal miner who exceeded his production quota in a very short amount of time. Section 3.3.

32) Known as the Great Purge, the people of the Soviet Union faced prosecution and little to no due process during the 1930s. During this time the period from _____ were the worst of the Great Purge years.

   A) 1917-1920
   B) 1937-1938
   C) 1940-1945
   D) 1945-1948

The correct answer is B:) 1937-1938. Another name for this period is Yezhovshchina which literally means the times or doing of Yezhov, who was the head of the secret police during that time. Section 3.4.

33) The major goals of Stalin's first five-year plan were _____.

   A) Socialization and capitalization
   B) Collectivization and industrialization
   C) Dekulakization and collectivization
   D) Mercantilism and free trade

The correct answer is B:) Collectivization and industrialization. Stalin attacked the kulaks, who were the farmers wealthy enough to own their own land, and he set goals and quotas for the nation's industry. Section 3.3.

34) The _____ emphasized the growth of heavy industry, increasing Russian steel production and improving communications and transportation. It also broadened the working class by introducing childcare to mothers who could then enter the workforce.

   A) First Five-Year Plan
   B) Second Five-Year Plan
   C) Third Five-Year Plan
   D) Fourth Five-Year Plan

The correct answer is B:) Second Five-Year Plan. Section 3.3.

35) The _____ from 1938-1941 was focused on producing weapons for the world war looming on the horizon.

    A) First Five-Year Plan
    B) Second Five-Year Plan
    C) Third Five-Year Plan
    D) Fourth Five-Year Plan

The correct answer is C:) Third Five-Year Plan. Section 3.3.

36) _____ was one of the most famous Russian film directors of all time, and his famous works were influenced by the concept of Soviet realism and important events in Russian history.

    A) Vsevolod Emilevich Meyerhold
    B) Maxim Gorky
    C) Anna Akhmatova
    D) Sergei Eisenstein

The correct answer is D:) Sergei Eisenstein. His revolutionary masterpieces are *The Battleship Potemkin* and *Ten Days That Shook the World*. Section 3.5.

37) Around _____ women served in combat alongside their male counterparts.

    A) 200,000
    B) 800,000
    C) 2 million
    D) 4 million

The correct answer is B:) 800,000. Section 4.1.

38) Prior to World War II, Russia was wary of German power and wanted to make alliances with _____ and _____, but those countries were not eager to pursue an alliance against Nazi Germany.

    A) Boston, Massachusetts
    B) Italy, Spain
    C) France, England
    D) Greece, Yugoslavia

The correct answer is C:) France, England. France and England were interested in appeasing Hitler rather than confronting him immediately before the war. Seeing as the nations were not interested in joining Russia against Hitler, Russia made a bargain with Hitler in order to gain territory. Section 4.1.

39) Between _____ Russian civilians died during World War II, bringing the nation's total losses to between 24-27 million people.

   A) 11-12 million
   B) 13-16 million
   C) 16-19 million
   D) 21-23 million

The correct answer is B:) 13-16 million. Russian civilians died from a variety of causes. Many were directly killed during the hostilities. Millions also perished from labor camps, illness, and starvation. Section 4.1.

40) During World War II, Russian forces suffered about _____ casualties between soldiers known to be either killed or missing.

   A) 200,000
   B) 4 million
   C) 11 million
   D) 24-27 million

The correct answer is C:) 11 million. This massive mobilization of forces and loss of life in combat had never been seen before in world history. Section 4.1.

41) The largest military offensive in world history was _____ against Russia.

   A) D-Day
   B) Operation Broken Arrow
   C) Operation Barbarossa
   D) Operation Typhoon

The correct answer is C:) Operation Barbarossa. The offensive involved over 4.5 million troops who attacked Russia over 1,800 miles. Section 4.2.

42) In 1939, the Soviets signed the Molotov-Ribbentrop Pact because they believed _____, and Stalin was trying to protect his country by forging an alliance with Hitler.

    A) The European nations would not come to Russia's aid
    B) Hitler would attack Russia
    C) Poland belonged to the Soviet Union
    D) Stalin opposed capitalism

The correct answer is A:) The European nations would not come to Russia's aid. The Russians were rejected by the Poles and by the Western European powers. Stalin was hoping to either avoid or delay conflict with Germany by forming an alliance. Section 4.1.

43) The Germans used a _____ to attack Russia during Operation Barbarossa.

    A) Two-pronged approach
    B) Three-pronged approach
    C) City-by-city
    D) Pierce and encircle

The correct answer is B:) Three-pronged approach. The German army was divided into the North, Center, and South Army Groups, and each group had a different objective. Section 4.2.

44) The military leader of the Russian army during World War II was _____.

    A) General Zhukov
    B) Premier Stalin
    C) General Molotov
    D) Tsar Nicholas II

The correct answer is A:) General Zhukov. General Zhukov's popularity among the Russian people would later save him from Stalin's jealousy and disfavor after the war ended. Section 4.2.

45) The Russian city of _____ endured a German siege for over 800 days.

   A) Stalingrad
   B) Kiev
   C) Leningrad
   D) Moscow

The correct answer is C:) Leningrad. This was the longest and costliest siege in world history. Over 500,000 Russians fought to defend the city along a front that stretched for over 300 miles. Section 4.2.

46) The Gulag had two purposes, to punish those who opposed the regime and to provide cheap labor, and Stalin's term for forced labor was _____.

   A) Patriotism
   B) Good stekhanovs
   C) Socially useful work
   D) Dekulakization

The correct answer is C:) Socially useful work. Millions of Soviet people died in the Gulag. Many simply starved to death or died of exposure, as the Gulag was not well supplied. Section 3.2.

47) May 9, or _____, is a sacred and important holiday to the Russian people because this is the date that they celebrate the end of World War II.

   A) Victory Day
   B) May Day
   C) Revolution Day
   D) Independence Day

The correct answer is A:) Victory Day. Over 20 million Russians died as a result of the Second World War. Section 4.3.

48) Germany invaded Russia on _____.

   A) August 23, 1939
   B) September 1, 1939
   C) June 22, 1941
   D) May 8, 1945

The correct answer is C:) June 22, 1941. This date signaled the initiation of Operation Barbarossa, the largest military operation that the world had ever seen. Section 4.1.

49) _____ marked the high point of collaboration between the Allied leaders before the end of the war.

   A) Yalta Conference
   B) Potsdam Conference
   C) Paris Conference
   D) Treaty of Portsmouth

The correct answer is A:) Yalta Conference. At the Yalta Conference, the Soviets promised to allowed democratic rule in Eastern Europe. Stalin also promised to enter the war against the Japanese in exchange for the return of Russian land. Section 4.4.

50) After _____ took command of the Wehrmacht in 1941, the distance between Hitler and the senior commanders widened, leading to combat ineffectiveness.

   A) Irwin Rommel
   B) Adolf Hitler
   C) Walther von Brauchitsch
   D) General Zhukov

The correct answer is B:) Adolf Hitler. Hitler became more distrustful of his senior commanders as the war progressed, and his decision would cost Germany in both personnel and materiel. Section 4.2.

51) _____ was the name given to the nations of Eastern Europe that fell under the Russian sphere of influence after World War II.

   A) NATO
   B) The Big Three
   C) The Eastern Bloc
   D) The Marshall Plan

The correct answer is C:) The Eastern Bloc. Section 4.4.

52) In 1945, Stalin implemented the fourth five-year plan, which focused on rebuilding the nation's _____.

   A) Consumer goods
   B) Heavy industries
   C) Eastern Bloc
   D) Freedom of speech

The correct answer is B:) Heavy industries. Stalin intended for his nation to become the leader in industry by 1960. Section 5.1.

53) The _____ was the plan that the United States proposed to rebuild Europe after World War II.

    A) Five-Year Plan
    B) Treaty of Portsmouth
    C) NATO
    D) Marshall Plan

The correct answer is D:) Marshall Plan. The Marshall Plan poured large amounts of American capital into the European economy. It also developed a close relationship between the European nations and Americans. Section 5.1.

54) In response to the military organization of NATO, the Soviet Union created a parallel military agreement for the nation under its sphere of influence called the _____.

    A) Warsaw Pact
    B) Treaty of Portsmouth
    C) Soviet Union
    D) Federation of Independent States

The correct answer is A:) Warsaw Pact. The Warsaw Pact came into existence on May 14, 1955. Section 5.4.

55) The first major conflict of the Cold War was the _____.

    A) Vietnam War
    B) Afghanistan War
    C) Korean War
    D) Gulf War

The correct answer is C:) Korean War. The North Koreans, supported by the communists in both Russia and China, invaded South Korea. Section 5.4.

56) _____ was the name given to the ongoing tensions between the nations under the Soviet sphere of influence and the western nations. This name was appropriate because the two sides never engaged in direct conflict.

- A) Vietnam War
- B) Cold War
- C) Korean War
- D) Proxy War

The correct answer is B:) Cold War. During the time of the Cold War, both sides were hesitant to employ their costly and deadly weapons systems. Most of their conflicts were fought through proxy wars. Section 5.4.

57) A _____ takes place when a conflict is encouraged by one nation against another, but the first nation never openly takes part in the hostilities.

- A) Vietnam War
- B) Cold War
- C) Korean War
- D) Proxy War

The correct answer is D:) Proxy War. There were many proxy wars during the Cold War. The war in Vietnam is a good example. Section 5.5.

58) The Economic Recovery Plan was the official title of the _____.

- A) Five-Year Plan
- B) Treaty of Portsmouth
- C) NATO
- D) Marshall Plan

The correct answer is D:) Marshall Plan. The plan took its informal name from Secretary of State George Marshall, who advocated for the plan. Section 5.1.

59) The _____ spurred the development of NATO when the communist government kept food and supplies from entering Berlin in 1948.

   A) Berlin Wall
   B) Berlin Blockade
   C) Siege of Leningrad
   D) Warsaw Pact

The correct answer is B:) Berlin Blockade. NATO became the military agreement that would unite the efforts of American and Western European nations. Section 5.4.

60) Under the guise of the Warsaw Pact, the Soviet Union intervened militarily in _____ when these countries tried to oppose Soviet rule.

   A) Hungary and Czechoslovakia
   B) Georgia
   C) Afghanistan
   D) Estonia, Latvia, and Lithuania

The correct answer is A:) Hungary and Czechoslovakia. The Soviets crushed the uprising and caused numerous civilian casualties. Section 5.5.

61) The proxy war between the United States and communist _____ would become very unpopular among the American public.

   A) Korea
   B) Vietnam
   C) Afghanistan
   D) Germany

The correct answer is B:) Vietnam. The American public disapproved of the war and returning veterans faced rejection by the American people. Section 5.5.

62) _____, the communist leader of China, at first seemed to benefit from Soviet support after World War II.

   A) Adolf Hitler
   B) Mao Zedong
   C) Chang Kai-shek
   D) Deng Xiaoping

The correct answer is B:) Mao Zedong. While Mao would at first receive aid from the Soviet Union, a rift would later develop between the Soviet Union and Red China. Section 5.5

63) Immediately after Stalin's death, _____ was in the highest office.

   A) Georgy Malenkov
   B) Nikita Khrushchev
   C) Joseph Stalin
   D) Lavrentiy Beria

The correct answer is A:) Georgy Malenkov. Although Georgy Malenkov was initially in power, he soon stepped down, leaving a vacuum. Section 6.1.

64) _____, who had been the head of the secret police, made a move to gain power, but was soon arrested and executed.

   A) Georgy Malenkov
   B) Nikita Khrushchev
   C) Joseph Stalin
   D) Lavrentiy Beria

The correct answer is D:) Lavrentiy Beria. Beria had begun to work to hide his involvement with many of Stalin's purges. Section 6.1.

65) Under Khrushchev, a quiet time of _____ began when people were able to return from prison camps, and some of the horrors of life under Stalin were revealed.

   A) Dekulakization
   B) De-Stalinization
   C) Cult of Personality
   D) Repression

The correct answer is B:) De-Stalinization. Khrushchev investigated Stalin's actions and revealed that many people had been unjustly imprisoned and executed. Section 6.2.

66) _____ embarrassed the Soviet people when he banged his shoe on the table at the United Nations.

   A) Georgy Malenkov
   B) Nikita Khrushchev
   C) Joseph Stalin
   D) Lavrentiy Beria

The correct answer is B:) Nikita Khrushchev. Section 6.3.

67) Khrushchev refused to participate in the _____ because the United States would not apologize for flying the U-2 spy plane over Russia.

   A) SALT I Negotiations
   B) Paris Summit
   C) Berlin Peace Treaty
   D) Warsaw Pact

The correct answer is B:) Paris Summit. Khrushchev did not want to believe that Eisenhower knew about the flyover. Section 6.3.

68) _____ wrote *A Day in the Life of Ivan Denisovich*, describing life in the Gulag.

   A) Boris Pasternak
   B) Nikita Khrushchev
   C) Aleksandr Solzhenitsyn
   D) Zhores Medvedev

The correct answer is C:) Aleksandr Solzhenitsyn. Solzhenitsyn faced exile from Russia, and his work was not published in his own country for decades. Section 6.5.

69) _____ was responsible for constructing the Berlin Wall in 1961.

   A) Walter Ulbricht
   B) Helmut Kohl
   C) Aleksandr Solzhenitsyn
   D) Adolf Hitler

The correct answer is A:) Walter Ulbricht. Section 6.4.

70) In the 1960s, the Chinese split with the Soviets because the Chinese believed that the Soviets were indulging in _____ because of the Soviet desire to peacefully coexist with capitalism.

   A) Capitalism
   B) Perestroika
   C) Counterrevolutionary trends
   D) The Cult of Personality

The correct answer is C:) Counterrevolutionary trends. The United States was relieved to see tension begin to appear between the two communist nations. Section 6.4.

71) _____ became the Marxist-leaning president of Chile in 1970, but he was overthrown by a CIA-sponsored military coup in 1973.

   A) Nikita Khrushchev
   B) Salvador Allende
   C) Francisco Franco
   D) Salvador Dali

The correct answer is B:) Salvador Allende. Salvador Allende would implement Marxist policies of nationalization and collectivization before he lost power. Section 6.4.

72) During the Suez Crisis, the United States and the Soviet Union objected to the invasion of _____ by France and Britain.

   A) Israel
   B) Hungary
   C) Columbia
   D) Egypt

The correct answer is D:) Egypt. Section 6.6.

73) The Berlin Wall fell in _____, although the official removal of the wall would not finish until the next year.

   A) 1981
   B) 1986
   C) 1989
   D) 1990

The correct answer is C:) 1989. Less than a year later, Germany was reunified. Section 7.5.

74) _____, a controversial figure, introduced the new policies of glasnost and perestroika.

   A) Joseph Stalin
   B) Leonid Brezhnev
   C) Nikita Khrushchev
   D) Mikhail Gorbachev

The correct answer is D:) Mikhail Gorbachev. Some see him as a visionary, while others think he was wedded to traditional communist ideals. Section 7.1.

75) Calling the Soviet Union an "evil empire," _____ consistently opposed the Soviet Union and hastened the end of the Soviet Union by continuing the arms race in America in the 1980s.

A) Jimmy Carter
B) Ronald Reagan
C) George H. W. Bush
D) George W. Bush

The correct answer is B:) Ronald Reagan. Ronald Reagan increased U.S. military spending while improving the U.S. economy after the economic struggles of the 1970s. Section 7.1.

76) _____ was a very different leader from his predecessor Khrushchev because he sought more consensus and rarely took action without first finding out how others felt.

A) Joseph Stalin
B) Leonid Brezhnev
C) Nikita Khrushchev
D) Mikhail Gorbachev

The correct answer is B:) Leonid Brezhnev. During some of Brezhnev's rule, the Soviet Union was able to make some important agreements with the United States, such as the SALT agreements and the Helsinki Accords. Section 7.1.

77) The policy of _____ encouraged more openness from the government and allowed more people to voice criticism of the government and its policies.

A) Glasnost
B) Perestroika
C) De-Stalinization
D) Disarmament

The correct answer is A:) Glasnost. Glasnost meant openness. Section 7.3.

78) _____ were two domestic policies proposed by Mikhail Gorbachev that hastened the end of the Soviet Union.

   A) Glasnost and nationalism
   B) Perestroika and glasnost
   C) De-Stalinization and democratization
   D) Disarmament and arms treaties

The correct answer is B:) Perestroika and glasnost. While Gorbachev hoped that these policies would give him the support he needed to improve the Soviet Union, the policies actually turned both the conservative and the liberal sides against Gorbachev. Section 7.3.

79) While in Ukraine, _____ gave a speech cautioning the Ukrainian people against nationalism because of the threat of Soviet reaction, and this speech would become known as the "Chicken Kiev" speech.

   A) Jimmy Carter
   B) Ronald Reagan
   C) George H. W. Bush
   D) George W. Bush

The correct answer is C:) George H. W. Bush. The speech had been written by Condoleezza Rice, who would later become the Secretary of State under George W. Bush. Section 7.6.

80) _____ was a strong leader and the only leader of an Eastern European country that stood up to Stalin and Cominform. Having helped his nation liberate itself from the Axis powers at the end of World War II with little help from Russia, this leader viewed himself as an ally with and not a subordinate to Stalin.

   A) Maxim Gorky
   B) Harry S. Truman
   C) Mikhail Gorbachev
   D) Josip Broz Tito

The correct answer is D) Josip Broz Tito. Tito developed his own brand of socialism that believed that each nation should be allowed to determine how best to implement socialist ideals within its own borders. This view was not popular in Moscow, and Tito was condemned as a follower of Trotsky. Section 5.4.

81) On March 11, 1990, _____ was the first nation to declare independence from the USSR.

   A) Yugoslavia
   B) Lithuania
   C) Poland
   D) China

The correct answer is B) Lithuania. When Lithuania asserted its independence, the Soviet Union said that the declaration was not legal because Lithuania had not followed the rules for secession in its constitution. Lithuania countered with the argument that the constitution was not legitimate to begin with because the Soviet rule had violated international law. Section 7.5.

82) The _____ was formed in opposition to NATO and mandated mutual aid if any one of the signatories was attacked.

   A) United Nations
   B) Soviet Union
   C) United Kingdom
   D) Warsaw Pact

The correct answer is D:) Warsaw Pact. The signatories were Albania, Bulgaria, Czechoslovakia, East Germany, Hungary, Poland, Romania, and the Soviet Union. The treaty disbanded after the fall of the Soviet Union. Section 5.4.

83) Regarded as an outsider, _____ was able to consolidate power after the death of Stalin and succeeded Stalin as the leader of the USSR.

   A) Nikita Khrushchev
   B) Vladimir Lenin
   C) Leon Trotsky
   D) Vyacheslav Molotov

The correct answer is A:) Nikita Khrushchev. Khrushchev possibly began his rise to power when none of Stalin's closest associates viewed him as a threat. Nikita Khrushchev was able to pit the other leaders against one another because Stalin had not designated any one person to take power after his death. Section 6.1.

84) The three _____ were the first nations to declare their sovereignty and reject membership in the Russian Federation after the Soviet Union dissolved.

    A) Baltic States
    B) German States
    C) Middle Eastern Countries
    D) Soviet Republics

The correct answer is A:) Baltic States. The three were Latvia, Lithuania, and Estonia. Section 7.4.

85) In response to the Russian invasion of Afghanistan, the Americans _____.

    A) Ordered sanctions against the Soviet Union
    B) Tore down the Berlin Wall
    C) Attacked Kabul
    D) Boycotted the Summer Olympics

The correct answer is D:) Boycotted the Summer Olympics. Carter's decision was controversial, as many athletes preferred to think that beating the Soviets would have had more meaning than not going to the games. Section 6.7.

86) _____ is the Russian word for restructuring.

    A) Glasnost
    B) Perestroika
    C) Dekulakization
    D) Collectivization

The correct answer is B:) Perestroika. This was a policy introduced under Gorbachev meant to improve the Russian economy. Section 7.3.

87) _____, the Russian vice president, was the leader of the coup d'état in 1991.

    A) Leonid Brezhnev
    B) Mikhail Gorbachev
    C) Boris Yeltsin
    D) Gennady Yanayev

The correct answer is D:) Gennady Yanayev. The coup lasted for a mere three days before Gorbachev returned to Moscow. Section 7.6.

88) _____ presided over the Soviet Union during the age of stagnation.

- A) Leonid Brezhnev
- B) Mikhail Gorbachev
- C) Boris Yeltsin
- D) Gennady Yanayev

The correct answer is A:) Leonid Brezhnev. Just as the rest of the world was facing economic difficulties during the 1970s, the Soviet Union's economy ground to a halt. Section 6.5.

89) Demokratizatsiya could not function without _____.

- A) Perestroika
- B) De-Stalinization
- C) Glasnost
- D) Capitalism

The correct answer is C:) Glasnost. Glasnost would allow the free circulation of ideas that would lead to criticism of the communist party as the sole party in the Soviet Union. Section 7.3.

90) The Afghanistan War cost the Soviet forces around _____ casualties.

- A) 5,000
- B) 14,000
- C) 20,000
- D) 100,000

The correct answer is B:) 14,000. The war in Afghanistan is viewed as the Russian equivalent to the American war in Vietnam. Section 6.7.

91) _____ was a period in the 1970s when the Soviet and American relationship was less tense and some agreements were forged.

- A) Détente
- B) The Thaw
- C) The Cold War
- D) The Afghanistan War

The correct answer is A:) Détente. Section 7.3.

92) _____ was the successor of Brezhnev, and the western powers were suspicious of him because he had been the leader of the KGB for an extended period of time before taking power.

A) Leonid Brezhnev
B) Mikhail Gorbachev
C) Yuri Andropov
D) Gennady Yanayev

The correct answer is C:) Yuri Andropov. Andropov would have a relatively short tenure in the highest office as he would die of kidney failure in 1984. Section 7.3.

93) The Russian leader, Stalin, used his influenced to prevent the Chinese from invading the island of _____.

A) Yalta
B) Formosa
C) Hawaii
D) Japan

The correct answer is B:) Formosa. Section 6.4.

94) The American relationship with the Chinese only began to improve after _____ made a secret visit to the nation in 1971.

A) Henry Kissinger
B) Condoleezza Rice
C) George H. W. Bush
D) Richard Nixon

The correct answer is A:) Henry Kissinger. Kissinger's visit would pave the way for Nixon's official trip to China in 1972. Section 6.4.

95) General _____ suggested that the nuclear bomb be dropped to cement a victory in Korea.

A) Dwight D. Eisenhower
B) Irwin Rommel
C) Douglas MacArthur
D) George S. Patton

The correct answer is C:) Douglas MacArthur. Along with insubordination, MacArthur also advocated for the use of the ultimate weapon to strike the final blow to the communists in North Korea. Section 5.4.

96) _____ became the first female prime minister of Great Britain and exerted pressure on the Soviet Union, leading to the dissolution of the USSR.

   A) Hillary Clinton
   B) Margaret Thatcher
   C) Queen Elizabeth II
   D) Raisa Gorbachev

The correct answer is B:) Margaret Thatcher. Known as the Iron Lady, Margaret Thatcher shared Ronald Reagan's views on communism. Section 7.1.

97) _____, a pope of Polish heritage, helped inspire the Polish Solidarity movement and urged the Soviet Union to allow freedom of religion.

   A) Pope Francis
   B) Pope John Paul II
   C) Pope Benedict
   D) Pope Joel Osteen

The correct answer is B:) Pope John Paul II. The pope even endured an assassination attempt while trying to spread his message of human dignity through freedom of religion. Section 7.1.

98) By driving the _____ religion underground, the Russian nation created a more fundamentalist strain of the religion in some of its socialist states.

   A) Russian Orthodox
   B) Christian
   C) Muslim
   D) Atheist

The correct answer is C:) Muslim. The existence of Muslim instruction underground built a new generation of radicalized leaders who were able to take power as soon as there was a power vacuum. Section 7.2.

99) _____ was the first Soviet leader born after the October Revolution of 1917.

   A) Leonid Brezhnev
   B) Mikhail Gorbachev
   C) Yuri Andropov
   D) Gennady Yanayev

The correct answer is B:) Mikhail Gorbachev. Gorbachev would soon be torn between the desire to enact reforms and the demands of hardliners who did not approve of reforms. Section 7.3.

100) _____ was a movement uniting Catholics in Poland against the Soviet-controlled government.

   A) Solidarity
   B) The Communist Party
   C) The Marxists
   D) Greenpeace

The correct answer is B:) Solidarity. This movement was able to win the first free elections held in Poland since World War II. Section 7.5.

 # Test-Taking Strategies

Here are some test-taking strategies that are specific to this test and to other DSST tests in general:

- Keep your eyes on the time. Pay attention to how much time you have left.
- Read the entire question and read all the answers. Many questions are not as hard to answer as they may seem. Sometimes, a difficult sounding question really only is asking you how to read an accompanying chart. Chart and graph questions are on most DANTES/DSST tests and should be an easy free point.
- If you don't know the answer immediately, the new computer-based testing lets you mark questions and come back to them later if you have time.
- Read the wording carefully. Some words can give you hints to the right answer. There are no exceptions to an answer when there are words in the question such as always, all or none. If one of the answer choices includes most or some of the right answers, but not all, then that is not the answer. Here is an example:

    The primary colors include all of the following:
    A) Red, Yellow, Blue, Green
    B) Red, Green, Yellow
    C) Red, Orange, Yellow
    D) Red, Yellow, Blue

    Although item A includes all the right answers, it also includes an incorrect answer, making it incorrect. If you didn't read it carefully, was in a hurry, or didn't know the material well, you might fall for this.

- Make a guess on a question that you do not know the answer to. There is no penalty for an incorrect answer. Eliminate the answer choices that you know are incorrect. For example, this will let your guess be a 1 in 3 chance instead.

 # Test Preparation

How much you need to study depends on your knowledge of a subject area. If you are interested in literature, took it in school, or enjoy reading then your study and preparation for the literature or humanities test will not need to be as intensive as that of someone who is new to literature.

This book is much different than the regular DANTES study guides. This book actually teaches you the information that you need to know to pass the test. If you are particularly interested in an area, or feel that you want more information, do a quick search online. We've tried not to include too much depth in areas that are not as essential on the test. Everything in this book will be on the test. It is important to understand all major theories and concepts listed in the table of contents. It is also important to know any bolded words.

Don't worry if you do not understand or know a lot about the area. With minimal study, you can complete and pass the test.

Legal Note

All rights reserved. This Study Guide, Book and Flashcards are protected under the US Copyright Law. No part of this book or study guide or flashcards may be reproduced, distributed or stored in a retrieval system, or transmitted in any form or by any means, electronic, mechanical, photocopying, recording, or otherwise, without the prior written permission of the publisher Breely Crush Publishing LLC.

FLASHCARDS

This section contains flashcards for you to use to further your understanding of the material and test yourself on important concepts, names or dates. Read the term or question then flip the page over to check the answer on the back. Keep in mind that this information may not be covered in the text of the study guide. Take your time to study the flashcards, you will need to know and understand these concepts to pass the test.

A Day in the Life of Ivan Denisovich	Berlin Blockade
Détente	Douglas MacArthur
Economic Recovery Plan was the official title of what?	Gennady Yanayev
Germany invaded Russia on what date?	Josip Broz Tito

Spurred the development of NATO when the communist government kept food and supplies from entering Berlin in 1948	Aleksandr Solzhenitsyn
Suggested that the nuclear bomb be dropped to cement a victory in Korea	A period in the 1970s when the Soviet and American relationship was less tense and some agreements were forged
VP, leader of the coup d'état in 1991	Marshall Plan
Socialist	June 22, 1941

Kolkhozy	**Korean War**
Latvia, Lithuania, and Estonia	**Lavrentiy Beria**
Mao Zedong	**May 9**
Nikita Khrushchev	**Perestroika**

First major conflict of the Cold War	Collectively owned farming associations
Head of the secret police	Rejected membership in the Russian Federation
Victory Day	Communist leader of China
Restructuring	Embarrassed the Soviet people when he banged his shoe on the table at the United Nations

Pope John Paul II	President of Chile in 1970
Proxy War	Sergei Eisenstein
Socially Useful Work	Solidarity
The Berlin Wall fell in what year?	The largest military offensive in world history

Salvador Allende	Helped inspire the Polish Solidarity movement and urged the Soviet Union to allow freedom of religion
The Battleship Potemkin	When a conflict is encouraged by one nation against another, but the first nation never openly takes part in the hostilities
Movement uniting Catholics in Poland against the Soviet-controlled government	Stalin's term for forced work
Operation Barbarossa	1989

The longest and costliest siege in world history	Walter Ulbricht
Warsaw Pact	Which two policies hastened the end of the Soviet Union?
Who called the Soviet Union an evil power?	Who gave the Chicken Kiev speech?
Yalta Conference	Yuri Andropov

Built the Berlin Wall	Leningrad
Perestroika and Glasnost	Created in response to the military organization of NATO
George H. W. Bush	Ronald Reagan
Successor of Brezhnev	Marked the high point of collaboration between the Allied leaders before the end of the war

NOTES

NOTES

NOTES

NOTES

NOTES

NOTES

NOTES

NOTES

www.ingramcontent.com/pod-product-compliance
Lightning Source LLC
Chambersburg PA
CBHW081832300426
44116CB00014B/2568